Praise for
AVERAGE MAN, ALMIGHTY COMPANION

In this rustic narrative, Bob eloquently presents his years of journaling to show his walk with Jesus amid a myriad of experiences from childhood through adulthood. He contrasts struggles in many areas of his life with euphoric mountain top experiences in his teens, marriage, family, vocation, and retirement. Bob weaves Bible verses to accentuate experiences and truths. I highly recommend this presentation of an average life lived under the newness, strength, and guidance of Jesus Christ.

- Ron Cook, Minister of Pastoral Care, King Street Church

I've known Bob for over fifteen years, and I can attest, he's the real deal! Average Man, Almighty Companion is an easy read. Bob's well-documented journey with God may well help you with yours!

- Rick Alexander, Operations Manager, Alpha Media

This is a down-to-earth book from a transparent Christian friend, who is honest, spiritual, practical, and humorous. You will find these pages to be an easy read, challenging, entertaining and by the first chapter riveting, like an LED light aimed right into your own soul. Walk to that light and not away from it. Be changed forever by the Lord of light, on your own spiritual journey.

- Doug Lichty, Pastor at Ironsprings Brethren In Christ Church

If discipleship can be defined as Christlike character transformation, then Bob has given us a wonderful glimpse into how his "Almighty Companion" continues to walk with him and mold his life's story. He humbly reveals to us that there are no "Average" Image-bearers in God's Kingdom. "From glory to glory," Amen.

- Reverend Mike Wentz

AVERAGE MAN, **ALMIGHTY COMPANION**

A Story and Playbook for Witnessing God's Presence in the Journey

AVERAGE MAN, **ALMIGHTY COMPANION**

A Story and Playbook for Witnessing
God's Presence in the Journey

ROBERT JONES

FOREWORD BY JOANNA SANDERS,
AUTHOR OF *FIRE WOMEN*

Copyright
Robert Jones, Chambersburg, PA
Copyright © Robert Jones, 2020
All rights reserved. No part of this book may be reproduced in any form without permission in writing from the author. Reviewers may quote brief passages in reviews.

2020
DISCLAIMER
No part of this publication may be reproduced or transmitted in any form or by any means, mechanical or electronic, including photocopying or recording, or by any information storage and retrieval system, or transmitted by email without permission in writing from the author. Neither the author, editor or publisher assumes any responsibility for errors, omissions or contrary interpretations of the subject matter herein. Any perceived slight of any individual or organization is purely unintentional.

All Scripture quotations unless otherwise indicated, are taken from the Holy Bible, New International Version®, NIV®. Copyright © 1973, 1978, 1984, 2011 by Biblica, Inc.™ Used by permission of Zondervan. All rights reserved worldwide. www.zondervan.com The "NIV" and "New International Version" are trademarks registered in the United States Patent and Trademark Office by Biblica, Inc.™

Scripture taken from the New King James Version®. Copyright © 1982 by Thomas Nelson. Used by permission. All rights reserved.

Cover Design: Propel Marketing LLC
Editing: Joanna Sanders LLC
Layout & Formatting: Propel Marketing LLC
Author's Photo Credit: Diane Jones

ISBN 978-1-7353972-0-7
ISBN 978-1-7353972-1-4 (eBook)

Dedication

To my amazing, loving wife, Diane: Thank you for loving me and standing by me for 35+ years of marriage. You are my best friend and number one cheerleader. Your life and example continue to draw me closer to Jesus Christ every day.

To my three wonderful daughters: Thank you for standing by me during the times when my career, responsibilities, tiredness, and other distractions often took first place in my life. You never complained about the times I was "there" but not "there". Despite all of the responsibilities and travel, somehow, I was "there" for you during every significant life event. I am so proud of each of you. I love you and pray that you experience the love of Jesus Christ each moment of your lives.

To my parents: Thank you for providing for me, supporting me, and loving me even when I was "unlovable."

To Rick: a celebrity and gifted speaker, and one of the most real, humble men I know. You are the person I could call at 2 in the morning and you'd pick up the phone. Thank you for your friendship, encouragement, and Godly example.

To Mike: a gifted pastor, musician, and friend. Thank you for your encouragement and timely words.

To Jeff: a great friend and former boss who gave me the opportunity to be a leader. Thank you for believing in me and for the lessons you continue to teach me.

To Joanna: For your patience, Godly character, expertise, and friendship. I thank God for bringing you into our lives to bless us and bring this story to fruition.

To Pastor Jody: Thank you for introducing me to the concept of the "Upper" and "Lower Story."

To a host of other "seed planters" who influenced and continue to influence my journey.

Contents

Foreword 11

Introduction.. 15

Chapter 1: The Upper and Lower Story 27

Chapter 2: Seed Planters.. 61

Chapter 3: Living a Life of Gratitude 73

Chapter 4: The Blessing of Miracles............................. 83

Chapter 5: Calling Out to God 95

Chapter 6: The Words We Speak 105

Chapter 7: Listen Up! 117

Chapter 8: A Husband, a Dad, and His Money 125

Chapter 9: Making the Most of Opportunities.......... 137

Chapter 10: Loving Difficult People............................ 147

Chapter 11: My Struggles with "Self" 157

Chapter 12: When You Get "That" Phone Call 183

Chapter 13: Decisions, Decisions 201

Chapter 14: Wake-up Calls 227

Chapter 15: Don't Give Up 247

Chapter 16: Where Do We Go from Here?.................265

About the Author...297

Foreword

WATCHING THE SUNRISE at the beach with a cup of coffee in hand is one of my very favorite things in the world. This, New Jersey, a mutual friend, and a couple other minor details, are the only things that the author and I had in common initially. We didn't grow up together. We didn't attend church together. We didn't go to the same school. Truthfully, we have never even met in person. I have not had years of knowing Bob's character. But I was one of the first ones to read through, with the blessing of his wife, many of his journal entries through the past three decades and to seek God's wisdom in formulating it into the book that you now hold.

Unlike me, I assume many readers will begin this book either having known Bob personally, or will have met him and had the privilege of him courageously handing them this book with a blessing. Others may find it online and never have a chance to shake Bob's hand in person. I am in a very unique position. It is quite an honor for a stranger to hand you their personal journal, and then trust you to prepare it for the eyes of the world to see, including the audiences that I just mentioned. I pray, for those of you that know Bob well, that you believe that I have honored God's story through him appropriately.

My journey with Bob as his editor, and now in friendship with him and his wife, has been unexpected and joyful. However, as a wife, myself, I found something different in this book than I've experienced in the many other manuscripts I've encountered.

I believe that the heart of a Christian wife is to intimately know the heart of her husband. In mirroring the relationship between Christ and his bride, I believe it is a beautiful reflection of how God made us to want to know His heart. While I don't use this word often, the "magical" thing about the book in your hands is that it gives you an intimate journey into a man's heart, his honest struggles, his failures, and his successes. Yet from the very moment I first connected with Bob, he was clear that he wanted none of the glory even for those "perceived successes." He only wanted his Companion to be seen.

As a wife, I tend to consider myself my husband's most precious companion. Which, if I'm honest, can often lead to difficulty when our sights don't completely line up. In this book, God reminded me that my husband has a more precious Companion on his own journey. And as I walk side-by-side with him, it is my honor to get a glimpse of the reflection of that. Views like this are intimate, and a precious gift from God. What Bob has done here, is the equivalent of him taking a long walk on the beach with you, and giving you a glimpse of the footprints that have accompanied his journey. Seeing the undeniable footprints on Bob's journey has reminded me how important it is to help my husband see those same footprints on his.

By the end of my interaction with this manuscript, Bob had inspired me to journal once more myself. I also found myself on a long hike, the day after I had finished my initial edit. And as I write this foreward, the sun is rising over the ocean on the beach and I am here, watching with cup of coffee in hand. My friend has inspired me to see the footprints of my own Companion all around me.

I extend my thanks to Bob and Diane, for allowing me into this good work, which I still don't feel like I deserve. But just like the sun rising over the beach each morning, God continues to take my breath away on the journey.

I pray that as you read this, you treat Bob's story with the intimacy he has entrusted into your hands. I pray that you receive and see it all through the eyes of grace and love, as we are all currently in the midst of our own journeys. I hope that you get some great laughter out of his hilarious stories. But more importantly, I pray that as you get to the end of your long walk on the beach with Bob, that you will understand, in your own way, that you have never traveled this journey alone. In God's sight, none of our stories are average.

Joanna Sanders
Editor, Friend, and Author of *Fire Women: Sexual Purity & Submission for the Passionate Woman*

Introduction

I N THE 1989-1990 TIMEFRAME, I HAD TRAVELLED NUMEROUS TIMES TO CHICAGO FOR WORK. Specifically, the work venue was in a Chicago suburb, just outside of O'Hare Airport. The routine was always the same: I would drive sixty-five miles from home to the airport in Harrisburg, Pennsylvania, for a direct flight to Chicago. On one of the last trips to Chicago in 1990, I left my house for the airport and stopped to pick up a colleague who would accompany me. As I waited for him to come out of his home, I checked to ensure that I had my airline tickets (back then you had to carry hardcopies), credit card, and my driver's license, since I would need it to rent a car in Chicago. Amazingly, you did not need to show ID at the airport back then!

The tickets and credit card checked out, but I searched my wallet inside and out and could not locate my license. I asked my colleague if I could use his house phone to call my wife, (no cell phones then). I thought that perhaps I had left it at home, although that would have been unusual. I am typically meticulous about those things, so I imagined there had to be another explanation. My wife searched the logical places in our home to no avail. I had no idea where my driver's license was and I needed to get to the airport.

I arrived at the airport, checked in, and eventually boarded the airplane. During the short flight from Harrisburg to Chicago, I obsessed over how I would rent a car without a license. I would either have to let my colleague rent the car, take a taxi, or walk to work. Then the thought dawned on me: *Since I was renting from a company we used continually, perhaps they would not require a license, and I could replace it after the trip. After all, the company should have my information in the system.* I had been there just a month prior to this trip. I convinced myself that this would work out if I played it cool, but deep down, I was still apprehensive.

The plane landed, and I took the shuttle to the rental car agency. I made my way to the counter and everything was going as planned. I thought I was home free with just a credit card, but then the dreaded statement came: "You're all set Mr. Jones, I just need to see your driver's license."

Uh oh. I am not a dancer, but I tried my best tap routine. Sheepishly I said, "I apologize, but I seem to have misplaced my license." Suddenly, a thought dawned on me, and I believe now that it had to be from the Lord. From out of nowhere, I blurted out, "It's not possible that I left my license here the last time I rented, a month ago?" Even as it came out of my mouth, the thought was preposterous, and I didn't think in a million years that this was possible. I figured that the taxi option or "walking" to the office would be my likely fate on this trip.

What happened next made my jaw drop. The clerk pulled out a cardboard box from under the counter and sifted through the contents. I watched as he picked my license out from among random office supplies, and handed it to me. He did not seem phased nor surprised, but I almost fainted. It was such a relief, but also miraculous. A million thoughts raced through my mind at once! *How did I not notice that the clerk never returned my license on the previous trip? And how did he not notice? Why did the company just keep the license and not mail it back to me, or call me? I drove around, unknowingly, for a month with no license? What if I had been pulled over? What if I had never returned to Chicago, to that rental car agency?* If I hadn't, I might still be wondering what happened to that license. It was buried in a box with miscellaneous items in Chicago!

As you will see, (from this, and several other stories I include in this book), I am not always the "sharpest knife in the drawer," but my faux pas make for good stories! I have accumulated a lifetime of stories based on more than thirty-five years of marriage to an amazing wife, the raising of three wonderful daughters, and worldwide travel experiences for business. I continue to learn not to take myself so seriously. I love a good story, and I love to laugh. I also enjoy occasionally poking fun at myself. Whether we realize it or not, each of our lives tells a story. Each of us is on a course for a destination, and our stories are being written, day by day, moment by moment.

Stories have played a significant role in my professional life as well. For more than a decade, I was in a leadership position in my first career, where I periodically had to speak in front of large groups. I made it a habit to use real-life stories and well-placed humor to articulate important points and sometimes "break the ice" with the crowd. These stories were not only effective in conveying a message, but intended to also show that I am a just an average, and rather imperfect guy. Employees and colleagues came to expect a good story whenever I held a meeting or had to brief an audience. More often than not, someone in the crowd would say, "Can we get a 'Bob' story today?"

I've learned that stories have power. Stories help us to remember significant events and ideas. Jesus often used parables (stories which provide instruction or lessons), as an effective tool to teach important principles to His disciples.

But I'm definitely not Jesus. I'm an average guy; a "nobody" to most people. With the name "Bob Jones" (I could write a book about the issues I've experienced because of my name); I am really just a face in the crowd. I am not a pastor, a Bible scholar, nor a counselor. I am a recovering pessimist, skeptic, and cynic. I've struggled with feelings of inadequacy, pride, anxiety, uncertainty, regret, guilt, and loss. I've worried about my marriage, children, career, finances, the state of our world, and what others think of me. I can put on a good front, and a happy face, but sometimes unseen battles rage in my mind. From my perspective, I have no tangible qualifications to be an author. Yet, I've watched the work kind of create itself.

The idea all started when I was contemplating retirement from my third career, in late 2019. I reflected on my life and thought about the daily habit of writing my thoughts down on paper. You see, over the years I've accumulated quite the stack of journals which have served as my "diaries."

I had started journaling in the early 1990s, right around the time I gave my life to Jesus Christ. I didn't realize how long I'd been writing until I placed the journals in a pile and the stack measured over a foot high! Journaling had become a regular activity as part of my daily quiet devotional time with the Lord. Through the years, I found this practice to be inspiring and therapeutic, especially during difficult times. There was something comforting about putting my thoughts down on paper. Journaling also provided an avenue for me to record historical world and family events through some very busy periods. Over the years I had filled thousands of pages with praises, requests, answered prayer, life events, random and deep thoughts, and history. And when I reflected on the patterns I saw through the pages, I realized it also gave me a record of how I'd grown spiritually.

I began to wonder if someone else out there would be blessed by the stories of how God had impacted my life. I considered that perhaps another husband, dad, employee, leader, or fellow citizen would be able to relate to some of my personal struggles and how I dealt with them. Yet the idea of writing a book still seemed preposterous. I am an introvert who originally wrote all of these thoughts for my own edification! I had no intention of ever placing intimate details about my own personal life out there for anyone to read. And to be honest, I'm still not comfortable with it! Yet I couldn't deny that I sensed the Holy Spirit pushing me to proceed.

When I mentioned the idea of a book to business colleagues and friends, I got positive feedback and I figured that perhaps it wouldn't be such a difficult task since I had everything already written down in the journals. Was I wrong! As you'll see in many of my stories, I'm a little slow learning important lessons! I planned to transcribe almost thirty years of journal entries into an electronic document. It didn't take me long to realize that I would be 100 years old before I finished! Consequently, I compiled a number of selected journal entries and recorded pertinent stories. It took a few months to put together, but something was missing with my original draft manuscript, so I reached out for help.

Thankfully, through a sister-in-Christ, God brought my writing coach and editor, Joanna, into my life. She involved both my wife and me to participate and go deeper into issues we've faced and how God had responded. The result is what you hold in your hands. It looks totally different from what I planned to write and turned out to be one of the hardest things I've ever done. I believe that this is the book I was supposed to write. And it all belongs to Him. Through this experience, I've learned a great deal about myself, and have grown closer to Jesus Christ. That alone has made this worth the effort!

Ok, Bob. We got it. You're an average guy. You're not so great at keeping track of your license. You wrote a million journal entries and you have some funny stories. But what difference is it really going to make in my life to read your book?

Ready for the bottom line?

There is an acronym I learned in my career as a manager. Leaders, especially those in senior management, typically do not have the time, nor desire, to read through the minutia contained in documents such as proposals or large briefings. For this reason, it was common practice for employees to furnish a "BLUF" to management, which synopsizes the detailed message. BLUF is the acronym for "Bottom Line Up Front."

The BLUF for this book is this:

Fix your eyes on Jesus and follow Him.

Why should this be important to you?

In sports, teams use playbooks for plans and strategies to win games. In business, playbooks contain plans for getting things done. The Bible has been my ultimate playbook which I rely on daily for instructions and encouragement. This book, my compilation of journal entries, stories and challenges, serves as a personal playbook to display how an Almighty God has worked in the life of an average man. To be sure, I have had a trusted Companion to guide me. You'll read more about Him as we progress in this book. I believe you have One too. I want you to see it as well. I want you to experience God in your journey. That's the bottom line.

As you read this book, picture yourself sitting across from me, perhaps having coffee or a meal, sharing life stories together. This book can be used as a devotional for men, but women may benefit as well by seeing a man's perspective on the issues and some of the challenges we face in life. Chapters are topical and contain selected journal entries and real-life stories where God has intervened and carried me in my journey. I show what I've learned through each situation. I also left space to record your own thoughts and prayer requests, how God has responded, and any changes you might need to make in your life to draw closer to Him. I would encourage you to highlight, underline, and make notes on principles you want to remember. I always have found it helpful to go back to my notes whenever I need encouragement in a life situation.

There is an old saying: "How do you know where you are going if you don't know where you've been?" Looking back at my journal entries, during good times and bad, I am reminded of God's love, goodness, and faithfulness. I am also encouraged and grateful for the miraculous, redemptive work He has done in my life. And He is not finished with me yet! If I had to summarize the contents into a sentence it would be, "God has been faithful in all situations." Things have not always turned out the way I desired, nor has God regularly answered prayers according to my specific requests. But He has been with me in all circumstances. I never would have gotten through the "storms" of life apart from His presence.

It's important for you to hear my story because it's true. I haven't exaggerated anything here because I planned to write a book. As I said earlier, the process has worked the opposite way. The truth is, my story is one of undeserved redemption. I was headed one way on my journey, and, thanks to my Companion, I'm now walking in a different direction. The Bible says this in 2 Corinthians 5:17:

> *Therefore, if anyone is in Christ, the new creation has come: The old has gone, the new is here!*

Jesus Christ, my Companion, totally changed my life.

My prayer is that everything in this book will point to the amazing love, grace, mercy, and glory of my Lord, Jesus Christ. Have Your way, Lord, and be glorified!

Thank you for reading, friend. I'm praying for you.

Gratefully,

Bob

Chapter 1: The Upper and Lower Story

For now we see only a reflection as in a mirror; then we shall see face to face. Now I know in part; then I shall know fully, even as I am fully known.
1 Corinthians 13:12

My pastor often preaches about an "Upper Story" and a "Lower Story." The Upper Story, he explains, is God working in ways that we cannot see, and the Lower Story is everyday life as we see and experience it. I love this analogy. I believe it reflects the reality of our perspectives. In my Lower Story, I have experienced everything from great joy, beauty, and miracles, to pain, grief, heartache, anxiety, and feelings of hopelessness. Although the

Bible gives us a glimpse of the Upper Story in this life, we won't have a perfect vision of it, until we see Jesus face-to-face.

Yet I've learned to trust even what I cannot see, despite my prayers not having always been answered in the ways or the timing I would have liked. I've come trust what He is doing in the Upper Story and I desire to fulfill His will for my life in the Lower Story. Why? Because I have seen the following Scripture proven true over and over again:

> *...we know that in all things God works for the good of those who love Him, who have been called according to his purpose.*
> *Romans 8:28*

My hope is that as you trek with me through some of my journeys, you too, will see my Companion at work in this very way.

Before we get into my journal entries and topical stories, I want to share how this average guy got here—my Lower Story. God has been so good to me in spite of the choices I've made and the paths I've travelled.

A Little Background

As I reflect on my life, it's a miracle that I even made it to this point. I feel like I've lived two separate lives, and, in a real sense, I have. There was life before Jesus, and abundant life *after* He rescued me. I was not "saved" as a child, nor was I raised in a Christian home. Truth be told, I was always a little jealous of brothers and sisters in Christ who have a testimony in which they gave their life to Christ as a child and have been successfully walking with Him for decades. My story is not even close. I took a circuitous route to God. In fact, at one point, I totally rejected Him.

Until I was about thirty years old, my life was characterized by self-centeredness, self-reliance, pride, and enough bad choices to fill many books. (Notice how the word "self" appears several times.) For the most part, I kept my sins hidden and they were not obvious to the casual observer. I could put on a good front but these character traits revealed themselves in childhood, adolescence, and adulthood. I got to the point in my life where I believed that I was too far gone for God to rescue me. A couple times during my college years I thought about "checking out," because I could find no meaning in life despite having accumulated a number of earthly accolades.

The Early Years

I grew up as the oldest of three children in a little working-class town outside of Philadelphia. We lived in a modest three-bedroom, one-bathroom, ranch house. I was a "normal" kid as far as "normal" was defined in those days. I walked to school, played sports, and had my share of injuries, (and scars) from doing things that boys do. When I was in third grade, I spent a week in the hospital with a concussion, which was obtained by falling from the top of a bunkbed. I have one scar from jumping on my parents' bed and coming down on the headboard. (Ouch! I'm glad I was too young to remember that one.) I have another one from a heavy Tonka truck that my younger brother threw at my head. I won't say that I deserved it, but I teased my brother continually and definitely provoked a response. Could too many blows to the head account for some of my peccadilloes? (I'm joking, but, maybe?) Another scar on my finger came from surgery to repair a break from when I decided to perform a flying leap off a playground sliding board. The sliding board won, by the way. These scars serve as a permanent physical reminder of some of the bad decisions I made when I was young.

Mom did not work outside of the home until us kids were in our teens. For as long as I can remember, Dad worked two jobs to provide for the family. Consequently, he was typically absent at home from dawn, until after 10 p.m. during the week. Dad's absence gave me license to frequently give Mom a hard time. Most of the time, she would not relay my shenanigans to Dad because her threat to do so usually set me straight. Normally the words, "just wait until your father gets home" caused me to rapidly shift my behavior. I was never quite sure if she would, or wouldn't, tell Dad. When she did tell him, or when I got too out-of-hand, I paid a price with my father. He was strict and commanded respect. I called him "Sir" well into adulthood, and he insisted that I refer to other male adults in the same way. There was no such thing as a "Time Out" for punishment for me. (To be honest, the threat of a "Time Out" back then probably would not have been an effective punishment for me anyway.) Fear was a pretty good deterrent to keep me in line, but not a tool that I brought into the parenting of my own kids.

Mom always tried to give me the benefit of the doubt when I misbehaved. She had an expression that I never forgot: "Rob, (that's the name my parents and siblings call me, even to this day), you need to turn over a new leaf." Truthfully, I turned that fictional "leaf" over so many times that it doubled as a pinwheel.

I picked up Mom's sensitivity and Dad's work ethic, stoicism, and temper. I am grateful for my sensitive side which I kept hidden as a young man because I was taught that "boys need to be tough." I am also thankful for my dad's work ethic which taught me personal responsibility and the rewards of a job well done. Unfortunately, I carried the obsession with work to extremes in my career, which caused times of stress and burnout. Thankfully, with my wife's positive influence, I taught balance to my three daughters. Each of them is industrious and conscientious, but they keep work in perspective. I always wished that I had inherited my dad's intelligence and sharp mind, but I think that these things must have skipped a generation.

Despite my behavior at home, I did relatively well in grade school and garnered the respect of most teachers. Outside of school, I found ways to get into mischief and had no filter on my tongue. As was true later in life, I could look like the model kid on the outside, but what was in my heart and in my thoughts were typically very different. Jeremiah 17:9-10 perfectly reflects this point:

> *The heart is deceitful above all things and beyond cure. Who can understand it? "I the LORD search the heart and examine the mind, to*

> *reward each person according to their conduct, according to what their deeds deserve."*

My mother's side of the family had Christian roots, but religion was not a part of our home life. To her credit, when I was a boy, Mom insisted that I attend Sunday School at a small Protestant church in town. I wasn't thrilled about going to Sunday School, but was taught the basic Christian concepts and stories. I attended church as a teen, sang in the choir, and made a confession of faith at age seventeen because it was expected. Truth be told, my life did not reflect my confession in any way.

My takeaway from church back then was one of legalism; God was a rigid taskmaster and my job was to obey and try to keep the Ten Commandments. For a while, I was actually afraid of God and tried to live an outwardly "holy" life. That didn't last long; it was impossible and frustrating to live that way. Back then, I knew nothing about the grace of God.

I loved high school when I first started in freshman year; new beginnings, new school, new friends. I was part of the music crowd and enjoyed Marching, Concert and Stage bands, along with Choir and Chorale. However, my self-esteem plummeted as a sophomore, when I developed severe acne which lasted for the better part of two years. I was extremely self-conscious of my appearance which caused me to withdraw. The girls who were interested in me during freshman year were nowhere to be found. Well-meaning kids and unthinking adults would come right out and say things like, "What's wrong with your face" or, "You really have a bad case of it, don't you?" Subsequently they often offered their medical remedies for the condition, as if I hadn't tried every acne and face wash product on the market. Not only did these comments hurt, but they also made me angry, and I kept it all bottled up inside.

By the time my parents sought a dermatologist for me, topical and oral medicine could only do so much. In order to reduce the size of the growths, I had to tolerate injections in my face and neck. Since the acne itself was painful, the shots were painful also. Eventually I got used to the injections since they were the only solution to reduce the large lesions. Ironically, the formal name for the condition is "acne vulgaris." Even though "vulgaris" is a Latin term which means "common," in my mind, there was nothing "common" about this acne! I dreaded looking at myself in the mirror.

By my senior year of high school, the worst part of the acne was gone, but I still dealt with skin issues even into the college years. I also carried emotional baggage and had difficulty figuring out who I was. I felt like a social outcast and was extremely insecure, self-centered, and cynical. When any girls showed the slightest interest in me, I jumped into a relationship with them. I was awkward and apprehensive about how to behave with girls, and did not treat them with the respect they deserved. I didn't take the time to get to know anyone I was dating. I didn't know what I wanted, and so with every young lady I dated, I wondered if "the grass would be greener" with someone "better." I acted foolishly and would break things off as soon as I felt like my needs were not being met. I had my heart broken a couple of times, but regrettably, and more often than not, I was the cause of pain in several relationships. And this pattern continued when I went away to college. Remember the physical scars I talked about? I have a few emotional scars as well, because of how I treated girls I dated. The scars are reminders of how heartless I was, but also how much I've since been forgiven.

The Band

I learned to play harmonica in third grade, and have loved to sing ever since I can remember. I have also played the saxophone since fourth grade, and continue to do so from time-to-time. I am grateful that my parents paid for private lessons which allowed me to excel on the sax in junior high, as well as high school. I played in a number of honors and regional bands and received several accolades. There were many more-deserving, talented musicians than I, but I loved to play. Music continues to be an integral part of my life and I consider it to be a wonderful gift from God.

When I was sixteen, my Uncle Joe obtained a guitar for me. It was a Fender Mustang, complete with a little amplifier. I had so much fun with that guitar! I took a few private lessons at the same school of music where I studied saxophone. My guitar teacher encouraged me to find a good band where I could play the sax and earn a little money for college. He invited me to play in his band at a New Year's Eve gig in Philadelphia. That was quite the experience for me as a sixteen-year-old playing with guys in their thirties! Even though the "drinking age" was eighteen in those days, I was "part of the band," so no one ever questioned me. Spending time in that environment opened my eyes to a whole new world.

Back in the '70s and early '80s there were many opportunities for musicians to play in nightclubs, social events, and weddings. There was an old saying that "any musician, good or bad, could find work on New Year's Eve." I found that statement to be true.

Back in those days, we didn't have internet, so I ran a personal ad in the local newspaper seeking a "working" band. After a few false starts, I joined an established band which played regularly on weekends. We played weddings, parties, and other social gatherings. This experience lasted for five years, until I graduated college. Playing and singing with the guys gave me a sense of identity, purpose, and meaning. The insecurity I felt in high school was replaced by a sense of acceptance, significance, and pride. I loved being with my bandmates.

The environment also led me into risky activities and behaviors which often come with the territory of playing in a band. I crossed lines without much thought for whether my actions were right or wrong. Honestly, with the risks I took then, I am seriously thankful to be alive. God spared my life and has been so patient with me. I don't understand, nor do I deserve His grace and mercy, but He saved me physically from harm and death. I would have been eternally lost had I continued with the lifestyle I led.

I never intended to go so deeply into sin but ended up there by a progression of actions. Once I crossed a line, just a little, it was easy to keep walking. I believed lies such as, "one drink won't hurt you," or "you're young, live a little, no one has to know." The problem was, it didn't end with one drink, or living a little. I wanted to live a lot. Feeling good and the comfort of acceptance overrode any risky behavior. I relate my progression of my thought life back then to that of King David when he sinned with Bathsheba (check out 2 Samuel 11). It all started with a look. If it had ended there, (for him or me), the story would have been different. But the look turned into desire, and things went downhill from there. Sometimes even today when I share a little of my story with others, I'll hear things like, "you weren't that bad," or "we all did things like that when we were young." I appreciate the empathy, but have also seen others' lives cut tragically short due to the consequences of risky behavior very similar to mine. God spared me. My story points to His mercy, not excuses for my youthful sins. Truly, God used my bad choices to eventually bring me to my knees. It took a while, but He never gave up on me.

College

I was a high school senior when I started playing music professionally. My band director and several friends suggested that I major in music in college. Yet, since I had no desire to teach music, and was already playing in a band, that major was not on my radar. I wanted to study a subject where I could excel and obtain good grades. I applied to, and was accepted into two colleges where I planned to study German. I had a phenomenal high school German teacher, and did well in that subject. I also felt like good grades on my transcript, regardless of major, would look better to an employer than average grades in a more "marketable" subject. For this reason, I chose to pursue German as my major.

Out of the two schools I applied to, one school was commutable and the other was two hours from home, located just outside of New York City. The farther school had a unique major which consisted of International Business coupled with a foreign language. This program seemed like a great ticket to post-college employment, so I chose the farther school to pursue the combined major of German and International Business. Moreover, I could not wait to get away from home, on my own, so I selected the more distant school. On most weekends, I still travelled home to play in the band.

As soon as I got to college, the first thing I did was ditch church and the idea of following Jesus Christ. I developed my own opinions about God and the meaning of life. When I was younger, I had viewed God as a judgmental supreme Being, ready to lower the boom on me if I stepped out of line. Now that I was in college, I completely abandoned that idea and took an opposite view of God. I believed in God's existence, but viewed Him as more of a loving, forgiving God who "graded on a curve." I knew nothing about His grace, nor did I think at all about the consequences of sin. Compared to others, I believed that I was basically a good person by my own standards. Proverbs 16:2 says,

> *All a person's ways seem pure to them, but motives are weighed by the LORD.*

This was totally accurate for me. I felt like I had many years ahead of me and that God would forgive me of my selfish behavior, how I treated girls in relationships, and the risky lifestyle I was living with the band. I reasoned that I was young and had time to get serious about God, someday. I didn't realize that I was only considering one aspect of who God is, and was playing a very dangerous game. I had a huge chip on my shoulder and felt invincible. I was living the independent life that I wanted to live; enjoying college life, and everything that came with it. I was playing in the band on weekends. Life was all about me, what I wanted to do, and what made me feel good. On the outside I was very "happy."

My dad used to say, "Rob, you've got the world by the tail," and I smugly sat back and believed it. In reality, I felt like I did have it made. Outwardly, I had everything going for me. College was the ticket to a lucrative career and a happy life, so I was told. I was also a professional musician and enjoyed all of the ancillary "benefits" that came with it, especially the praise and recognition. I lived for the weekends when I knew I would be with the guys, up on the stage. But, when the people left, and the stage was empty, so was my soul. I can still remember how it felt when the music was over. When I put my head down on the pillow late at night (or early the next morning since gigs sometimes ended after midnight), I had a hollow feeling and wondered, "so what?" The music and band were not the problem, but my identity was wrapped up in those things. No one close to me knew or could understand what was going on in my head.

I would sometimes ask myself the question, "Is this all there is?" In one form or another the basic questions of life would haunt me, such as, *Who am I? Where did I come from? Why am I here? Where am I going?* I didn't have any good answers. I didn't really know who I was, that I was created by a loving and holy God, that He had purpose for my life, and that I was headed on a path, straight for eternal separation from Him. I hated thinking about those questions and just lived for the next "high."

Good people would tell me things like, "you need to find your own way and follow whatever works for you" or, "once you get your college degree you'll find meaning and significance." I also heard, "once you get a stable career and get married, you'll be happy." But each time I accomplished a significant goal or realized a milestone, something inside of me said, *Okay, now what? Is this what "happy" feels like? I want my money back.* So, most of the time I kept as busy as I could to avoid giving those thoughts more attention.

In addition to the band, during summer college breaks, I worked in two different factories doing manual labor jobs. It was hard work, but rewarding at the end of the day. I helped to produce products that were tangible and I made a nice wage doing it. My dad and mom demonstrated intense work ethics and I followed. I eschewed summer vacations and fun for money.

It amazes me how much we are influenced by our surroundings. I learned a great deal working in those factories, including a variety of new vocabulary on the job. Profanity and crude joking were an inherent part of the environment and used so much by coworkers, that it didn't take long for me to pick up the lingo. (Ironically, my parents used the occasional curse word in their daily speech, but I didn't dare use profanity at home. My dad did not tolerate foul language from his kids, but he had no idea what my language was like outside of the home.) My circle of friends didn't consist of people who were close to Jesus, or who would have cared about my profanity either. I knew some followers of Christ in college but avoided them based on earlier assumptions from my past experiences with church. I hung out with people who were like-minded and agreed with my interests, and the things I was doing.

In college, I was taught to ask questions, examine issues thoroughly, and not draw premature conclusions based on incomplete information. Ironically though, I was "dug in" on my opinions about God, without bothering to consider alternative views. My experience with church growing up and my college way of thinking made me skeptical about religion, especially when it came to Christianity. I was judgmental and ignorant.

Despite my avoiding them though, the questions kept coming, and the search for meaning eventually led me to seek answers anywhere I could. *What is my purpose in this life? What will make me happy? What if there is no God and we're just random, insignificant people? Why does Jesus Christ have to be the only way? What about all of the other religions, how can they all be wrong?*

As part of the Honors Program in college, one of the benefits was a $25 stipend per semester to a local bookstore. I wasn't much of a reader until college but I used this "bennie" to purchase and read every self-help, religious, philosophical, psychology book I could get my hands on. For whatever reason, I avoided the Bible and any "Christian" books. My church experience had been too restrictive and I wouldn't live that way. I had learned about characters like Noah and Jonah in Sunday school, via picture books and flannel easels. But these were just cute little stories in my mind and had no basis in reality. Moreover, I found the Bible difficult to understand, and consequently avoided the investigation of its claims.

The more I read in these other books, the more I felt like I knew it all. The quest for knowledge gave me a sense of pride and superiority. In reality, I didn't know much of anything. Proverbs 3:7 says,

> *Do not be wise in your own eyes; fear the Lord and shun evil.*

I was definitely wise in my own eyes. Had I held on to my misconceptions, I would have been eternally lost.

I did discover some truths in all of the teachings I investigated and took some superficial satisfaction in that. I discovered that many religions, philosophies, and ideologies taught values which aligned with Christianity, such as love others, perform good deeds, treat people with respect, care for the environment, etc. I was able to rationalize some sinful behaviors when a particular belief system validated them. However, I couldn't find absolute truth or permanent meaning in any belief system I investigated, and at the end of the day, none of these worldviews filled the void in my soul.

I also didn't find lasting satisfaction in possessions, accolades, or relationships. I wish that I had known about the book of Ecclesiastes back then. I think that King Solomon was onto something in the second verse of Chapter 2:

> *"Meaningless! Meaningless!" says the Teacher. "Utterly meaningless! Everything is meaningless."*

That was my secret perspective as I went through the motions of life in my college years. As I continued running from truth, I dreaded placing my head on the pillow at night. It was a lonely, dark place, especially in my college dorm room and rest did not come easily. On weekends when I returned home from a band gig in the wee hours, normally amped up from the experience, I couldn't sleep. I would sleep in until Sunday afternoon and wake up feeling wrecked from the night before. After a few hours home, I would make the two-hour drive back to school. Sunday nights in my dorm were especially depressing. I figured that there had to be more to life but I didn't know what. Once Monday morning rolled around it was back to class and things were "okay" in the routine for the week. I looked forward to the next weekend. In reality, I was on a hamster wheel and couldn't get off. But I didn't want to, either. God was merciful to sustain me through these times.

I graduated college in May 1983 with honors and hope for new beginnings. I had finally destroyed an "on again, off again" relationship that I had all through college. I didn't want to be tied down, and never saw myself getting married anyway. My dream was to find a high-paying, prestigious career where I could work in the city, live on my own, and play in the band. New York or Philadelphia would have been just fine.

Unfortunately, the job market was not favorable for hiring that year. It was a stressful time because my parents pressured me my entire senior year to search for a job. I floated numerous resumes around which resulted in only a handful of interviews. This was supposed to be the beginning of my bright future. *Would my dreams be shattered? Now, where would I find meaning?*

In June of that year, I felt fortunate to be accepted into an intern program for a large organization. But there was a catch: the position was in Texas. A move from New Jersey to Texas, in the heat of July, was not part of the plan. I was happy to have found employment, but everything unfolded quickly and I was not looking forward to the move. It would rip me out of my comfort zone and I was certain it was not the dream that was going to make me happy.

I did receive one other job offer in another part of New Jersey, but it was for a temporary position. It would have involved finding a place quickly, in an expensive area, but I was still interested since the job wasn't in Texas. Thankfully my father would have none of it, and insisted that my destiny was etched in stone. "You shall go to Texas to secure the best future for your life." My parents threw a big surprise "going away" party for me a few days before departure. I was not the best company at that soiree. Leaving the "known" for the "unknown" was hard.

I didn't know it back then, but this was God's perfect plan. He was working the whole time in the Upper Story, in spite of me, and I'm forever grateful. While this was going on, there was a young lady in northern Pennsylvania who had graduated college in 1982, but could not find a job in her field. She worked in a retail department store for a year before being accepted into the same Texas intern program.

The "Lone Star" State

I started my first career in Texas, in late July 1983. Dad packed up his small Nissan and made the two-day trip with me from South Jersey to Texas. Looking back, I'm not sure how we fit everything, including my guitar, into that small car! They say that Texas is hot in July, but it was even hotter than I expected. I found the people of eastern Texas to be welcoming and friendly, though. To this day, despite the heat, I remember Texas fondly.

Dad put a down payment on a new vehicle for me with the condition that the payments and insurance were my responsibility. Making the down payment to get me started was very generous of my dad. Mom flew down shortly thereafter, and both parents helped me get set up in an apartment. I am grateful to this day for my parents' presence and financial boost as I started this chapter of my life. Based on their kindness, I did the same type of thing for my daughters when they moved out to pursue their first careers.

Mom and Dad stayed with me until I completed my first day of class. When I returned that first day, they said their goodbyes and left for the long drive home to New Jersey. This may seem insignificant, but I need to mention it because it was one of several catalysts which gradually softened my hard heart. As I said goodbye to my mom and dad and hugged them, my mom cried, which I fully expected. What I did not expect, was seeing my dad cry, which set off the water works for me. This was the first time I had ever seen my dad cry. Dad was the toughest guy I knew, and to see him cry just rocked my world. I was taught that men didn't cry. When I cried as a boy, my dad had no sympathy for me when I was upset, so I did my crying in private, even as a teenager. When I was about 12 years old, his dad, Grandpop Jones passed away and I didn't remember seeing him cry then. I had never seen that emotion from him and I didn't know how to process it at the time.

On my first day of class in Texas, I met the young lady to whom I referred previously, Diane. I don't know if it was "love at first sight," but we hit it off from the moment we met. Out of a class of forty people, Diane sat directly behind me. We started talking when she overheard me saying that I had lived on the East Coast, and we never stopped talking after that.

One thing led to another. After a week, we were dating, and within three months, we were engaged.

Talk about taking things slowly and carefully! As I said before, I had a lousy track record with relationships, but this one was special. Still, the "Bob" who did not treat girls with respect made a few appearances while we were dating, and I almost blew it a couple of times. Thank God, Diane never gave up on me. The thing that was different from other girls I had dated, the thing that I loved (and still do), is that we had so much to talk about. She is outgoing (something I'm not by nature), beautiful inside and out, and has a wonderful sense of humor. I wanted to know everything about her. Despite my past, and myriad of character flaws and bad choices, she saw something positive in me. She brought out the best in me, and continues to do so. To this day she remains my absolute best friend.

God is so amazing with His perfect timing. If one, or both of us had been attached, or if either one of us had taken a job somewhere else, we would have never been together. Diane has had the most profound influence on my life. If there is such a thing as a "soulmate," she qualifies as mine. It scares me to think of where my faith would be had it not been for Diane.

It didn't happen immediately, but her influence watered previously-planted seeds, and gradually drew me back to Christ. Diane was raised Roman Catholic, and I as a Protestant. During our time in Texas, we visited several churches, both Roman Catholic and Protestant denominations. Diane was a true follower but I was just a "fair weather fan" of God. I didn't know it at the time, but she had received Jesus Christ at a revival service at a friend's church while in junior high school. I claimed to be a Christian when we were dating, but I did not "walk the talk." Things would change after we were married and had our first child.

Back to the East Coast

At the completion of our internships in 1984, Diane and I were assigned to an organization in central New Jersey. We worked on the same floor, but in different areas of a large six-story office building. Shortly after relocating to New Jersey, we were married, and settled into a routine, which did not include church. I felt like after working hard all week with a sizeable commute to the office, the weekends belonged to *me*. Saturdays were for errands, and work around the house. Sundays were for sleeping in, reading the newspaper, watching sports, and enjoying a good meal. Sometimes we would drive to South Jersey and visit my folks. On other weekends, we would drive to Pennsylvania to visit Diane's parents. Over time we visited a few churches, but did not commit to anything. Two years later, our first daughter was born.

It's an understatement for sure, but things do change when you have a child. (I was blessed to be there for the births of all of our children and I cried tears of joy every time.) The beauty of this precious new life planted a desire in me to find a church. I wasn't following the Lord, but I wanted my child (and later children), to be raised in the church and lead good, moral lives. I wanted to set a positive example for my children, and didn't want them to make the mistakes I had made. I reasoned that maybe they would not make the same bad choices I did, if they were raised in the church.

We settled on a little country church which had a Protestant label, but similar practices to the Catholic Church which Diane was accustomed to. The messages made me feel good, but were not particularly convicting. Truthfully, anything more challenging likely would have turned me off to church. I figured that attending church was good "fire insurance," tantamount to checking off a box. After church service was over, I felt like I had done my duty for God, and was "covered" for the week. I lived as I pleased during the week. There was no Bible reading, no prayer life, no journaling. I found my significance in the job and it often competed with my family for first priority in my life.

Diane became a stay-at-home mom once our first daughter was born. We made the decision together and tried to save as much money as we could, while she was still working. With an hour commute to work we felt like there wouldn't be sufficient time, nor energy, to spend with our daughter if we chose the route of childcare. It was a struggle financially, but we managed, and lived on the frugal side. Central New Jersey is not the cheapest place to live, but we felt like we didn't lack anything we needed. Looking back, these were good years as we lived a very simple life.

Several years later, a new job opportunity arose for me in central Pennsylvania. The region had a lower cost of living than New Jersey, which was attractive, and we could relocate to an area which was about a two-hour commute from Diane's parents. We had difficulty selling our home in New Jersey at first, and lived in a small apartment for several months before moving into our new home in Pennsylvania. Initially, I wondered if the move wasn't the best decision, but things worked out. We lived in a very rural area and it was the perfect place to raise a family.

We planned to have a second child, but Diane miscarried. This was a traumatic experience for her and myself. We were not sure if she could have another baby, so we just hoped and prayed (mostly she prayed). God did eventually bless us with a second, and later, a third child. Then, in 1990, there existed the strong possibility that my job would be dissolved. We were new to the area, with no extended family immediately nearby, and a thirty-year mortgage to pay. What were we going to do?

It was a stressful time and caused me to question life again. *Why did we move here? Was I being punished for my sins, and the way I had treated God, and others?* I know that people go through much worse, but this was my crisis. Ultimately, I was reassigned within the same organization and God eventually blessed us with two more daughters. The waiting was hard but it did teach me to be more patient. As a good friend and former boss continually said to me, "All's well that ends well."

What I didn't realize at the time, was that God was working in the "Upper Story" all along to draw me to Himself. The circumstances in the "Lower Story" brought me from a posture of questioning, towards a position of total surrender. I didn't admit it outwardly but, deep inside, I began to realize how little control I had over my life. This wonderful life I had planned for my family could come crashing down at any time. I needed God, but wasn't quite "there" yet.

Things came to a head in the early 1990s when I learned that my great uncle had passed away. Uncle Fred was my maternal grandmother's brother. He lived with my grandparents in southern New Jersey, close to where I grew up. Uncle Fred was a reserved, somewhat stoic man, but extremely wise. He seldom talked about himself and cherished his solitude. Like my maternal grandfather, Uncle Fred would always make time to sit and talk with me when I came to visit. He imparted practical wisdom which I carry with me to this day. Towards the end of his life, he suffered physically and could not have visitors. When he ultimately passed into eternity, it hit me hard—but God would use this event to change my life forever.

Shortly after his death, my maternal grandmother (Nana), planned a small memorial service for Uncle Fred at a funeral home in southern New Jersey. The service was small and limited to family only. Diane and I packed up our two small children and travelled from Pennsylvania to New Jersey the night before the service. We stayed overnight in a hotel which backed up to the New Jersey Turnpike. Prior to leaving, my grandmother called and asked if I would give the eulogy. I reluctantly agreed. I had no idea what I would say and was uneasy in my spirit. I hardly slept that night in the hotel. What inspirational words or platitudes could I offer? Did Nana think that I was living a Christian life and was somehow qualified to offer comfort to the family? I would have given anything at that point if someone else had stepped up to speak at this service.

Early in the morning of the service, I awoke and quietly left the hotel room while my wife and children were still sleeping. I walked outside to the back of the hotel and watched the cars zip by on the turnpike. It was a cloudy, dreary morning; quite depressing as I recall. My mind was in a state of chaos and I felt an unbearable emptiness. I could not fathom that someone I was so close to, was no longer on this earth. In my world, I did not think about the reality of death and it overwhelmed me to do so. The questions I wrestled with in college came back to me. *Is this all there is? Or, is there something beyond this life?* The tangible things I had put my faith in, including my job, my home, and my dreams didn't hold any meaning for me. *Why was I feeling this way now?* Life was going so well.

Standing there, confused, lost, and wondering how I would get through the service, I sensed God speaking to me in a clear voice. What I heard so vividly was this:

"I love you but you are not living for Me. Tomorrow is not guaranteed. If you die apart from Me, you will not

spend eternity in My presence. Why won't you surrender and give your life to Me? Isn't it time to stop running from Me?"

I was frightened and simultaneously convicted because I knew that these words described my current state exactly. At the same time, I sensed the overwhelming love and patience of a God who was still pursuing me in spite of my selfish, destructive past. I began to weep right there along the busy highway. I knew that I had to make a decision to live life differently. God had brought me to this point and was giving me a second chance in life.

Through my tears, I prayed and begged God for forgiveness, and asked for His help to turn from my sins and to follow Him. I had no idea what I was doing, but I knew that I wanted Jesus in my life, more than anything. I asked Him to come into my heart and save me. The Sunday School lessons and things I learned as a child came back to me: *God was real and loved me so much that He sent His Son Jesus to die for my sins.* I realized that I had not only sinned against others but also against God, Himself. He not only made forgiveness available on the cross, but also rose from the dead. *This life is not all there is. Because He lives, I can live eternally with Him. Death is just a transition into new life with Jesus!*

My life was transformed at that moment and I experienced joy and peace in my soul like never before.

Based on this miraculous encounter with the Lord by the turnpike, God gave me a message for my family at the eulogy. I am not a preacher, but I had a testimony and a story to tell, and I couldn't wait to tell it. I was rescued from a life of sin and eternal separation from God! This life is so short but there is good news in the Gospel. ("Gospel" literally means "Good News!")

> *For God so loved the world that He*
> *gave His one and only Son, that*
> *whoever believes in Him shall not*
> *perish but have eternal life.*
> *John 3:16*

Uncle Fred knew Jesus Christ as his Savior, so I rejoiced in the fact that his passing was a transition into eternity with God. While I still miss him to this day, I know that I'll see him again.

Matthew 10: 32 – 33 says this:

> *Whoever acknowledges Me before others, I will also acknowledge before My Father in heaven. But whoever disowns Me before others, I will disown before My Father in heaven.*

On June 26, 1992, at a Billy Graham crusade in Philadelphia, I went forward and made my confession public. I needed to publicly declare that Jesus saved me and that I intended to live for Him. I didn't care what anyone else thought when I went forward because I couldn't contain the joy of knowing Him. Receiving Jesus Christ as my Lord and Savior was the first step in this journey, and it changed everything for me.

When God rescued me on the morning of my great uncle's funeral, it was the beginning of an adventure that continues to this day. Like a marathon or a difficult hike, there have been many "ups and downs." But Jesus has made all of the difference. He is the reason for my hope. Hope, redemption, and love comprise the message which is woven throughout my journals and this entire book. God orchestrated everything in my life to draw me to Himself. I am still far from perfect, but God steers me in the right direction when I fall. As the result of my conversion, I had a new desire to read the Bible and God made it come alive for me. I've read through the entire Bible several times and make it part of my quiet time every day. This is how my Upper and Lower stories merged.

I hope that my story does not come across as some religious invitation or dialogue. That is not my goal. My story isn't about religion at all. I tried "religion" when I was younger, but I missed the grace of God, His unmerited, undeserved favor and love. No wonder the late John Newton wrote his famous hymn after God turned his life around. It really is "Amazing Grace!" My story isn't about a church either. Anyone can sit in a church but not know the amazing grace and love of Jesus. Jesus Christ, God Himself, is interested in a relationship with us which is an indescribable, wonderful, unfathomable blessing. My goal as a friend, is to simply tell you that I was a hopeless, undeserving beggar, and here is where I found food.

How long I will continue on this earthly journey, I do not know. But I do know this: I didn't get here by myself. I had an Almighty Companion, and He used (and continues to use) other people to draw me closer to Him. I call these people "seed planters."

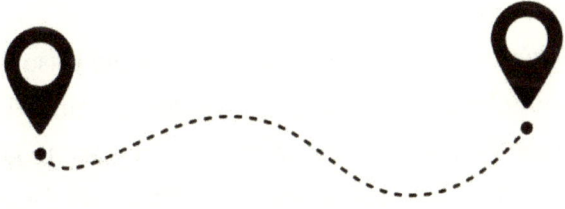

Chapter 2: Seed Planters

Two are better than one, because they have a good return for their labor: If either of them falls down, one can help the other up.
Ecclesiastes 4: 9-10

MAKE A POSITIVE INFLUENCE ON EVERYONE YOU MEET. Those were the words that Mr. O'Brien, my high school Psychology teacher, wrote in my yearbook. I don't remember much about psychology, but I remember two things about this man. First, was this important statement that he wrote in the yearbook which sticks with me still today. Next, was the requirement for his class. Each student had to learn how to juggle three tennis balls successfully in order to pass his course. Yes, you read that correctly. Amazingly, every student learned. I can still juggle today.

Oddly enough, I learned a couple valuable lessons from juggling. First, learning to juggle reminded me to focus on the task in front of me. It is so easy to get distracted or attempt to "multitask" which I found does not work; you end up giving a mediocre effort to multiple tasks rather than full attention to what is important. (Kind of ironic that learning to juggle taught me not to multitask!) Learning to juggle also taught me the need to learn a skill, to practice, and perfect it. I took these lessons into adulthood. I honestly didn't remember Mr. O'Brien until I started to write this book, but in our short intersection, he had a positive impact on my life. He planted a seed which I carried into family, business, and personal relationships.

In 1 Corinthians 3:6-7, the Apostle Paul uses the metaphor of a "seed" to describe the growth of the Gospel and the church. In these verses Paul tells us,

> *I planted the seed, Apollos watered it, but God has been making it grow. So neither the one who plants nor the one who waters is anything, but only God, who makes things grow.*

I love metaphors and I especially appreciate this one as I believe it applies to each of our lives. God uses people on our path to plant and water "seeds" in our lives, just like He did in the short time that I crossed paths with Mr. O'Brien. Seeds that are planted when we're young impact how we grow as we mature. As a result of the seeds planted, and how they are watered, we can produce healthy or unhealthy fruit.

Plenty of people planted both good and bad seeds in my life. Sadly, I allowed the watering of bad seeds to take root and precedence in my younger life. Yet God is able to prune us and produce healthy fruit in us as we submit to Him. Praise be to God that He used people to plant and water the good seeds, and then He miraculously made them grow, while simultaneously pruning me!

One of my earliest memories of both a literal and figurative seed planter in my life was my beloved grandfather, "Pop." Pop planted a large garden every spring, without fail. If there is such a thing as a "green thumb," I am convinced he had one. The seeds he planted in the early spring always resulted in a bounty of fruits and vegetables by summer. He cared for the soil, watered the seeds and plants, ensured that there was ample sunlight, and the Lord did the rest. Insects must have simply respected his garden because I never noticed any loss or damage; the plants always grew beautifully and flawlessly!

Pop's gentle, caring spirit carried into his relationships and had a profound influence on my life. From the time I was a boy, until he passed away in 1997, Pop always made time for me, no matter what he was doing. He would totally focus on talking to and listening to me. I believe that if cellphones were around back then, Pop would have turned his off and left it in the drawer when I came to visit. The fact that I was that important to him, that he would drop whatever he was doing to spend time with me, taught me that I needed to give my full attention to people. The seeds Pop planted in my life took time to grow into healthy fruit, but his influence remains with me to this day. Character traits such as empathy and compassion were not part of who I was originally, but they are part of who I am now, in no small part thanks to Pop's "seeds" and how God grew them over the years.

Pop was a principal seed planter in my life but there were many others whose influence made me into the person I am today. Parents are primary seed planters for their children, and mine certainly were for me. They weren't perfect, but none of us can claim to be. I certainly am not a perfect parent—I can only hope to plant seeds that will produce positive growth in my own children. Over the years, when I learned of my parents' own upbringings, their humble circumstances, and the times in which they lived, I at least understood some of the motivation behind how I was raised. Time, perspective, and above all, my relationship with Jesus Christ have minimized any negative memories and drawn me close to my parents. I am grateful for each day that I have them.

As you learned from the previous chapter, my parents were hard-working and dedicated. Even though I grew up in a small blue-collar town in southern New Jersey, my dad worked two jobs to provide for the family. For that reason, we always had a roof over our heads and food on the table. Mom and Dad also gave me the opportunities to pursue music, college, and ultimately a career. Above all, my parents taught me personal responsibility and the value of hard work.

While God was not a big part of my upbringing, seeds were planted that would produce good fruit later in life. I grew up with the notion that "no job is beneath me", i.e., give it your all regardless of the task. Whether I delivered newspapers, worked in a factory, pumped gas (which they still do at service stations in New Jersey), played in a band, or worked in an office, I gave it my "all." I didn't realize until adulthood that this is biblical wisdom, (assuming you're working with the right motivation and balance with other life priorities). Colossians 3:23 states,

> *Whatever you do, work at it with all your heart, as working for the LORD, not for human masters.*

What I love about this, is that even though my parents might not have realized that they were planting biblical seeds in me, God had them do just that by their positive example. God doesn't need our permission to use any of us as "seed planters!"

Another powerful seed planter was Aunt Mae. She was Pop's sister, and my great aunt. Aunt Mae was a godly woman who prayed continually for my salvation. I didn't know much about her, but she always had a smile on her face. Peace and joy were very evident in her life. When I was a young man, she gave me a Bible, which I still possess. She wrote this note inside the front cover of the Bible: "This book will keep you from sin, and sin will keep you from this book."

Those words didn't mean much to me back then but the seed was planted. Sin did keep me from reading the Bible, but these days "The Book," keeps me from sin. I can only hope to explain to her when I see her again in Heaven someday, how very much this small seed impacted my life.

Mr. Murray and Mr. Dunlap were two other men that should be noted for their impact and their good "seed planting."

Mr. Dunlap was a Sunday School teacher who invested in me as a boy. I have no idea if he is still on this earth, but his interest in me planted a seed which would later mature in my life. It was a radical idea (especially at the time), but Mr. Dunlap brought a portable basketball court into our Sunday School classroom. This turned the heads of church leaders for sure! When a student would answer a Bible question correctly, they earned the opportunity to take a foul shot. If they made the shot, they received a prize. Needless to say, I read my Bible lessons eagerly because I wanted to take the shot in class! Significantly, I can also recall a Saturday afternoon when Mr. Dunlap took me to the local recreation center to shoot hoops. It didn't mean much back then, but, the fact that a Sunday School teacher would take a Saturday afternoon to spend time with a student, planted a seed. While I don't recall the Bible lessons from that time, I do remember this lesson: Relationships are important to God and worth our time. Because of seeds like this, I developed a desire in my heart to love, encourage, and invest in people.

Mr. Murray, my high school German teacher ended up being one of the most profound seed planters in my life and I actually had the opportunity to tell him how grateful I was for his impact on my life at a recent reunion.

The fact that our paths even crossed is a miracle from God in my mind. Our district had two high schools. The closer school to my town was three miles away. The more distant high school was ten miles away. Which do you think I attended? (You've probably already sensed that I tend to stray off the beaten path.) Most students from my junior high, including the friends I grew up with, attended the closer high school. Unless there were extenuating circumstances, students were obligated to attend the school closest to where they lived. The only way one could deviate to the other school was if they signed up for a technical class such as Auto or Wood Shop, or a foreign language such as Italian or German. I still don't remember the exact reasons, but I did not want to attend the closer school. I only remember that it was an older school and I think I wanted something different. So, I signed up for German, which was totally foreign to me (see, I warned you about my sense of humor. Please don't stop reading, it's an acquired taste). The choice for German class automatically assigned me to the more distant school.

Mr. Murray was not only the German teacher, but also the head of the Foreign Language department. His expertise was actually in French, but his demeanor and teaching method attracted me to the German language. From day one, I knew that he was someone special. As it turned out, I studied German for all four years of high school and went on to get my college degree in the subject.

Mr. Murray had a way of investing in each of his students and showed a compassion that influenced my choices in higher education. His character molded me professionally in terms of leadership and people skills. It wasn't long before I had developed a love for the language, due to his passion for German and compassion for people. The difference one person can make! Don't ever think that your encouragement and positive influence on just one person will not bear fruit in the future.

God's Response and What I've Learned:

God used many other people to plant and water seeds in my life—many seeds which would not germinate until adulthood. Some seeds produced really bad fruit, especially in my teen and early adult years. But God used some amazing people along the way to plant and water seeds which eventually produced good fruit. Some of these seed planters have left this earth, and most, if not all, may not even realize the impact they had on my life. I thank God for each of these seed planters and the way God used them to ultimately bring me closer to Him.

Stop for a moment and think about the seed planters who influenced your life. I'm sure that you can name one, or many, who planted and/or watered those seeds. Maybe it was a family member, friend, teacher, or a seemingly "random" person. You'll be amazed when you give this some thought and recall those seeds which have blossomed in unexpected ways.

We encounter many people in this journey of life. It amazes me how people can come in and out of our lives, yet leave a mark of which they would never be aware. I believe that we can have either a positive or negative influence on each person we meet and with whom we engage. Be aware that God can use anyone, believer or non-believer, to plant seeds in your life. God also uses circumstances to help us grow. As we journey with Him, He can use anything in our path.

I want to spend my remaining days as a "seed planter", with my family, friends, coworkers, and "everyone I meet." I know that God has planted that desire in my heart; I see the proof of this pattern even in my journals:

September 12, 2000 (In Utah)

This will be the first full day here. I praise and lift up the Name of Jesus, my Lord and Savior. Thank You for bringing me here safely. Thank You for the answer to prayer, the opportunity to share the Gospel with two of my colleagues. I am amazed at how You open doors, Lord. I pray that Your words, not mine, will penetrate hearts with truth and that people would come to know You, if they don't already.

As I go into this day at work, around a lot of people, I ask for strength, wisdom, and power to lead a pure and holy life, that You would shine through my life and draw many to Yourself. I praise and thank You for all of this, in Jesus' Name, Amen.

God's desire is for us to be seed planters, as well as to experience His seeds being planted in us by others! This is one way His Kingdom grows on earth.

How about you? Can you recall the seed planters in your life? Are you yourself a seed planter? Do you look for ways to make a positive influence on those you meet? It's never too late to start. Take my Psychology teacher's advice, and make it a point to have a positive influence on everyone you meet. Imagine the garden you'll impact for God.

> *Do nothing out of selfish ambition or vain conceit. Rather, in humility value others above yourselves.*
> *Philippians 2:3*

> *In the same way, let your light shine before others, that they may see your good deeds and glorify your Father in heaven.*
> *Matthew 5:16*

Who are the "seed planters" in your life?

What impact have they had on your life?

What changes do you need to make?

Chapter 3: Living a Life of Gratitude

I will give thanks to you, LORD, with all my heart; I will tell of all your wonderful deeds.
Psalm 9:1

M**Y FAVORITE TIME OF DAY IS MORNING.** It wasn't always that way. Back in my band playing days, I was a night owl. Often, I would get home after midnight and sleep until noon the next day. These days, I now find that I turn into a pumpkin by 9 p.m. Mornings are fresh and new for me now. No matter what happened yesterday, the new day brings hope. I love to wake up just before dawn and watch the sunrise with journal, Bible, devotionals, and a good cup of coffee in hand.

My absolute favorite activity at the beach is observing the morning sunrise over the ocean waves. I grew up in New Jersey, less than an hour from the ocean, but I didn't care for the beach back when I was younger. I hated the smell of suntan lotion and was constantly annoyed by sand stuck to different parts of my body. Thanks to my wife and kids, we spent many vacations on East Coast beaches and I gradually grew fond of vacationing at the shore. (As an adult, I also discovered non-scented sunscreen which changed my life!) I just love watching the sun come up while enjoying the pounding of waves, and the ocean breeze, and, typically, the cup of coffee in hand. There is something miraculous, new, and unique every morning as the sun appears over the horizon. It's a wonderful time of day to commune with the Lord and marvel at His awesome creation!

This quiet, intimate time with the Lord is so precious to me that I equate it to physical food. I feel spiritually "hungry" if I ever miss this special time each day. Jesus seemed to like the morning for His quiet time as well. In Mark 1:35, it says this:

> *Very early in the morning, while it was still dark, Jesus got up, left the house and went off to a solitary place, where He prayed.*

If you've never tried it, I highly recommend that you intentionally set aside at least a few minutes each day to listen to the Lord. Spend time in God's Word and in prayer, away from the crowd, in a quiet place. Recording a few thoughts in a journal will also help you to document and remember what God is saying to you during this time. You will be amazed at the joy and peace this simple practice will bring you. I've found that if you do something as a routine for a few consecutive weeks, it will become a habit. It takes a little sacrifice and intentionality, but the joy and rewards are inestimable.

This personal practice helps to steady me for the rest of the day. In full confession, I struggle with "worry," in spite of God's faithfulness and my head knowledge of all the Bible has to say on the topic. You may not recognize it just to look at me, but my wife knows this all too well. My mind continually wants to go to a place of worry and anxiety. It could be a gorgeous day and I feel well, but my thoughts say, *what if (fill in the blank) happens today? Will I get an unexpected bill? Is the pain I have something serious? Are my kids having a good day? Will something happen with my parents?*

I trust God and recognize His goodness and faithfulness to me, so it's frustrating that my mind goes through this anxiety. I've found one powerful way to counter it—and that's where gratitude comes in for me. Starting the day with gratitude is the best way I have found to mitigate worry and the "what ifs" that come to mind. It might not be a total panacea for worry but I've found that gratitude provides the proper perspective to proceed with my day efficiently.

With all of the "baggage" in my thought life, I have to be intentional about focusing on the things God wants me to focus on. When I document blessings in my journal, it creates a permanent reminder of His goodness, for me, and hopefully future generations. I also go to the Scriptures to set my thoughts in the right place, which is on Jesus. When I go to the Lord in prayer, with a grateful heart, He provides a peace that is indescribable. Philippians 4:6-7 are verses I speak continually and have committed to memory:

> *Do not be anxious about anything, but in every situation, by prayer and petition, with thanksgiving, present your requests to God. And the peace of God, which transcends all understanding, will guard your hearts and your minds in Christ Jesus.*

The very next verse is also key to setting my mind in the right place. Philippians 4:8 says:

> *Finally, brothers and sisters,*
> *whatever is true, whatever is noble,*
> *whatever is right, whatever is pure,*
> *whatever is lovely, whatever is*
> *admirable—if anything is excellent or*
> *praiseworthy—think about such*
> *things.*

I have heard stories of other people who use a "blessing box" to record the things for which they are grateful. When the person recognizes a blessing from God, they write it on a slip of paper and drop it in the box. Later, perhaps when going through a difficult time, the "blessings" are reviewed as a reminder of all God has done. Sometimes it helps me to list all of the blessings God has bestowed on me. I don't deserve any of them, but He is gracious. He is the Giver of all good things. And I can prove it. I have many of the reminders from my Almighty Companion on the journey, including thousands of entries from my journals. Here are just a few.

March 25, 2000:

Gracious Heavenly Father, I praise You for who You are: Creator, Redeemer, Sustainer of Life, Friend, Giver of all good things, Righteous, Holy, Awesome Lord.

May 15, 2000:

Thank You Jesus for another day. Another day to be alive and to do Your will.

February 4, 2007:

I am thankful for the following:

1. You love me
2. You created me
3. You sustain my life
4. You provide for me
5. You have forgiven my sins and shown me grace and mercy
6. You speak to me and allow me to speak with You
7. You help me to accomplish things I can't do
8. You have given me a loving wife
9. A loving family
10. Friends
11. A job which provides for our needs
12. Shelter and food
13. Health

July 17, 2016:

It's just us, Lord. Thank You for the gift of this gorgeous new day. Lord, how can it be that among billions of people You can love me and hear my prayers? It is too much for me to comprehend. Among the noise and distractions, and the turmoil in our world, please let me hear Your voice. Have Your Way, and come Lord Jesus.

God's Response and What I've Learned:

No matter how I feel, I try to start out the day with a grateful heart for all the Lord has done. Sometimes I struggle with headaches or my mind is filled with concerns or tasks at hand. It's so easy to focus on the negative things we see around us. The simple discipline of beginning the day with gratitude helps to focus my mind on the Lord and His goodness. I have learned to take the time to center myself each day in this way.

The first part of Psalm 46:10 says,

> *Be still, and know that I am God.*

When I am still before Him, I recall all that He has done. Above all, He rescued me from a life of sin and eternal separation from Him. That fact alone fills my heart with gratitude. I have also learned to be grateful for the obvious things I take for granted: the beauty of a sunrise, a child's smile, the fact that I have breath, and could get out of bed this morning. Gratitude reminds me of His faithfulness and gives me hope whether I'm on the mountaintop or in the valley.

Worry puts trust in circumstances and "what ifs," and not the Lord. Worry says, "I won't trust what I can't see." But based on Philippians 4:6-7, God has promised peace when I come to Him with my prayers and petitions, with a thankful heart. Even during times of physical or emotional pain, expressing thanksgiving to my Lord always fills me with His peace.

When I set my mind on the things of Christ, with a grateful heart, it doesn't mean that worry and anxious thoughts won't creep in, but it focuses my mind where it belongs: on my wonderful, loving, gracious, Lord and Savior, Jesus Christ!

> *But I will sing of your strength, in the morning I will sing of your love; for you are my fortress, my refuge in times of trouble.*
> *Psalm 59:16*

What are you grateful for?

Consider an area that you've worried about. How has God responded?

What changes do you need to make?

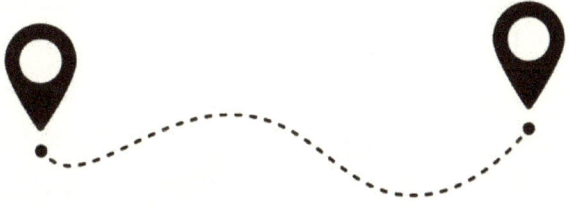

Chapter 4: The Blessing of Miracles

He is the one you praise;
He is your God,
Who performed for you those great
and awesome wonders you saw with
your own eyes.
Deuteronomy 10:21

I was on a two-week business trip to San Joaquin, California. Since my family wasn't with me and I had a free weekend with no plans, a friend suggested that I check out Yosemite. The national park was about two hours from where I was staying. I didn't know anything about Yosemite, but had nothing better to do, so I headed there. When I arrived at the park entrance, I asked a ranger for his recommendation on where to go and what to see. He suggested that I drive a few miles to a specific parking area and go from there. As I drove through the wooded area, it reminded me of a state park close to my home in Pennsylvania. I silently wondered what the big draw was all about. As I drove, I was listening to a Christian radio station and after several miles, came to a tunnel. As I exited the tunnel, the song "Majesty" (written by Martin Smith and Stuart Garrard) was playing. At that moment, the majestic granite mountains came into view. It was truly breathtaking and brought me to tears. I was drawn closer to God at that moment seeing the majesty of the mountains and the beauty of His creation, while the perfect song for the occasion played in the background, as if He had cued it, Himself. I pulled off to the side of the road in awe of the miraculous moment God created just for me.

At the time this book was written, I'd been following my Lord and Savior Jesus Christ for almost three decades. In that time, I've seen God do amazing, unexplainable things which I would characterize as genuine "miracles." (I view a miracle as an extraordinary event which can only be explained by God's intervention.) By that definition, I have seen so many miracles that a book could not contain them all. How can I explain the beauty and uniqueness of a sunrise, the majesty of mountains, the cascading of a waterfall, the birth of a baby, or trees blossoming in the spring? In beautiful irony, the Bible also says the same of the miracles that Jesus performed on Earth—that neither they could be recorded, even in all of the books in all of the world (John 21:25).

The Bible does record a number of miracles Jesus performed during His ministry on Earth. He healed diseases, brought dead people to life, fed at least 5,000 people with a few fish and loaves of bread, and cast out demons, to name a few. His first recorded miracle was described in John, chapter two, where Jesus miraculously turned water into wine. Interestingly, at the end of the story in John 2:11, it says this:

> *What Jesus did here in Cana of Galilee*
> *was the first of the signs through*
> *which He revealed His glory; and His*
> *disciples believed in Him.*

I believe this verse gives us a unique view of at least one reason why Jesus performed miracles. First, the "sign" (translated "miracle" in the King James Version), revealed His glory and His deity. Second, it caused His disciples to believe in Him because of it.

People seem to be attracted to the idea of miracles and supernatural phenomena. In Jesus's time, people were drawn to Him by the miracles He performed. But it was clear that some followed Jesus around for the miracles themselves, not because they genuinely loved Him. If I'm not careful, that can be true of my heart, also. I can come to expect that He will do something miraculous, *based on my terms*, to heal a hurt, relieve a painful situation, or provide something that I really want. I'm so thankful that He *has not* given me everything I've asked for in this life. In my opinion, the focus should not be on the miracle itself, but rather on God. The miracles can draw us close to Jesus in recognition that He is God, Himself.

Had the scribes of the Bible not recorded Jesus's miracles for us, how many of us would believe? If He used miracles then as a way to inspire us to believe, and know that He is God, I believe it is still important to recognize the miracles He performs personally in each of our own lives today. Recording a few of my own has served to remind me that God is not only in control, but can do absolutely anything. Nothing is impossible or too difficult for Him!

Unknown Terrain

During a snowstorm several years ago, I was driving to work in the darkness of the morning on a two-lane, snow-covered road. As I approached a curve, two vehicles occupied the oncoming lanes. I wasn't sure if the one approaching head-on was trying to pass, or if something else was going on. I had no choice but to bail to the right, into a field of unknown terrain. Somehow, I landed on all four wheels and my vehicle, a Jeep Liberty, did not flip over. Neither vehicle stopped to see if I was okay. I thanked God for sparing my life and wondered if I would be able to get back on the road. Miraculously, there was no damage to the car, and I was able to continue my commute to work, shaken but grateful. Days later, when the snow had melted, I visited the scene during daylight hours. The road had a pronounced drop off into the field where my vehicle landed. Logically, my Jeep should have rolled over given the terrain and the snowy conditions that morning. Call it what you want, I know that it was a miracle from God.

Angels Among Us?

In December of 1989, my mother was facing serious colon surgery and extremely anxious about the upcoming procedure. The night before she was to be admitted to the hospital, my wife and I spent some time with her. She was apprehensive about what the surgeon would find, and did not look forward to the pain and long recovery. As much as my wife and I tried to say the right things, no words could provide comfort to my dear mother.

Mom was admitted to the hospital the following day in preparation for surgery on the subsequent morning. That evening, Mom was visited by a woman who appeared to be a nurse. The visitor had a dark complexion, a large braid on top of her head, and was dressed in white. She came in with an open Bible and never identified herself. There was something about this woman that brought peace to Mom during this anxious time. This woman held Mom's hand, prayed with her, and assured her that God was present and everything would be okay. The woman's presence and reassurance superseded any comforting words we had spoken to Mom on the previous evening.

After the successful surgery, Mom thanked the hospital staff and specifically expressed her gratitude for the nurse who had visited and comforted her on the previous evening. She said that the visit was instrumental in giving her strength to get through the surgery. Surprisingly, no one on the hospital staff could identify the woman when Mom described her. To this day, no one knows the identity of the mystery woman who comforted Mom in a supernatural way. I praise God that she was there to minister to my mother in her time of need.

Was this woman an angel? I have no idea.

Was she sent from God? I absolutely believe so. He cares for us in an intimate way and comforts us in our times of need.

> *Are not all angels ministering spirits*
> *sent to serve those who will inherit*
> *salvation?*
> *Hebrews 1:14*
>
> *God is our refuge and strength, an*
> *ever-present help in trouble.*
> *Psalm 46:1*

The Tire

After the birth of our third child in 1995, we did what many American families did at that time: we purchased a minivan. When I was a youth, my parents bought a Ford LTD station wagon which could carry larger families. I guess that the minivan became the modern-day station wagon.

Our Ford Aerostar could hold up to seven passengers and we needed that space for my family of five and my parents. In September of 1998, I drove my wife, kids, and parents to a family christening in New Jersey. The trip went well and we travelled over 300 miles in total. When we arrived back home in Pennsylvania on Sunday, my parents said "farewell" and drove back to their residence in Virginia.

On Monday morning, I opened our garage door and got into my car to drive to work. I looked over and noticed that the van had a flat rear tire. This caught my attention, so I exited my vehicle to take a closer look. My jaw dropped as I looked at the tire, or what was left of it. The tire had two discernible vertical gashes and the tread was worn down to the steel belts. How we did not have a blowout on our trip, travelling at high speeds on the interstates, I cannot explain. My entire family could have been wiped out, and I shudder to think about it even now. God had His hand on my family and performed a miracle!

My journal entry based on that event:

September 29, 1998:

The Tire – We spent a long Monday night last night dealing with a flat tire on the van. But when I saw that the tire had two big gashes and was worn down to the steel, I wondered how we made it home on Sunday. We travelled over 300 miles with seven of us in the van. It could have been a disaster.

I remembered praying for a safe trip and having faith that the Lord has His hand on us. Did He! I don't know how that tire got us home but I know He, Who made all things, got us home. Thank You, Lord, for Your protection.

Pop's Miracle

I spoke about "Pop" in the "Seed Planters" chapter. He was such a wonderful grandfather and I miss him to this day. Nana and Pop lived in the same two-story New Jersey house until they could no longer deal with climbing stairs. In their later years, my grandparents moved to a home on Mom and Dad's property in southern Virginia. I always admired Nana and Pop for that step of faith. I couldn't imagine how difficult it was to leave the home they had lived in since they were married.

In early 1997, my mom called and told me that Pop was not doing well. He was in a local Virginia hospital and was weak and unable to speak. I made the 5+ hour trip with the two oldest girls to see Pop one last time. Deep inside, I knew that Pop had given his life to Jesus Christ, but I wanted to be sure. I had no idea if he would be able to hear, or even recognize me, but God allowed him to not only recognize and hear, but to speak for the last time. I'll let my journal entries tell the story.

January 4, 1997 10:05 pm in Virginia:

Drove down to see Pop today. Pop is sick and in the hospital. Given his condition and his age, it is likely he is dying. I didn't know what to expect when I would see him. I prayed that the Lord would help me handle whatever I would encounter. I also prayed for the opportunity to share Jesus. The Lord answered my prayers in so many ways.

Pop did not look good but when the opportunity came to share the Word, he listened. I read from John 1. When I asked Pop if he knew Jesus he said, "I think so." I said, "Pop, you can know for sure." I asked him if he believed that Jesus died for his sins and rose again. Pop could barely speak, yet I believe through the Holy Spirit he said, "I believe He was risen in three days and Lord, come into my heart." I then prayed with him and laid hands on him. He asked that I pray for an aunt which we did. I also prayed for Nana who announced that she had a relationship with Jesus.

Pop really enjoyed seeing the girls. We reconnected memories. A peace came over Pop, and Mom was touched.

January 7, 1997

Diane just called me at work and told me that Pop passed away. I pray for Mom and Nana. I pray for Dad, for strength. I'm thankful that I knew Pop, and thankful that I got to see him with the girls one last time.

God's Response and What I've Learned:

Do miracles still happen? Absolutely. God has taught me through the one-time miracles, and the ones I see every day, that He loves me, He is good, He hears my prayers, and is in control. I've also learned that when I hear His voice and He calls me to act (e.g., going to visit Pop while there was still time), I must do so immediately. I mentioned my Uncle Joe in an earlier chapter. He passed away in early 2020. When I learned that he was ill, God inspired me to make the journey to New Jersey to visit him, and share the love of Jesus. God blessed that visit for myself and my uncle. I heard Uncle Joe's confession of Jesus Christ and I now know that my uncle is in the glorious presence of his Savior. Don't miss those opportunities. You won't regret it!

We must be careful not to fall in love with the miracle itself, but to praise and worship Jesus Christ, the source of the miracle. In this world, we will have trouble and prayers don't always get answered the way we want. But He has always walked with me through every circumstance, good and bad. James 4:8 says,

> *Come near to God and he will come near to you.*

He has been an Almighty and Faithful Companion for me on the journey. And sometimes these miracles provide a most beautiful example of His presence.

What miracles can you identify in your life?

How has God responded to other times when you prayed for a miracle and didn't receive it? How did you feel about His response?

What changes do you need to make?

Chapter 5: Calling Out to God

In the morning, LORD, You hear my voice; in the morning I lay my requests before You and wait expectantly.
Psalm 5:3

I WAS ON MY WAY TO UTAH FOR WORK WHEN THERE WAS A SERIOUS SOFTWARE ISSUE IN MY COMPANY. I was responsible for a major project and the problem that presented itself was significant. A number of people, including myself, could not determine a solution and deadlines were approaching. I was early in my career and management was not happy with me. I journaled this entry on the plane:

March 21, 1995:

On my way to Utah.

A lot of potential work problems facing me. I've been called at home and the problems have eaten in to my family life. Trusting in You, Lord, for Your guidance, direction, and sustaining grace.

When I arrived in Utah and conferred with other experts, we tried a number of different solutions to no avail. That evening, lying in my hotel room feeling extreme pressure, I lifted up my problem to God, something I should have done in the first place. As I was praying, literally crying out to God, a thought came to me out of left field and I recognized that it would be a simple solution if true. It had to be from God because the answer was not in an obvious place. The theory turned out to be correct, and the problem was solved.

Some may get the idea that followers of Christ have everything figured out. If that's the case, then I'm doing something wrong, as hopefully you've been able to discern by now through my stories. I still struggle, and have questions at times. He is God, I am not. His ways are much higher than mine. I don't have all of the answers and often do not understand why something is happening. However, I take comfort in remembering that in every situation, whenever I've called out to God, He has answered. Usually the answer does not come according to my timing, or even how I expect. But looking back from the other side, He has always been faithful and has never failed to respond in some way. In fact, I'll go so far to say that He has answered and provided miraculously! My Almighty Companion has proven that He always hears my prayers and He desires that I commune with Him on the journey.

In my study of the Bible, I have found several Scriptures which I view as personal invitations to call out, even cry out, to our precious Lord:

> *Come to Me, all you who are weary and burdened, and I will give you rest. Take My yoke upon you and learn from Me, for I am gentle and humble in heart, and you will find rest for your souls. For My yoke is easy and my burden is light.*
> *Matthew 11:28-30*

> *The righteous cry out, and the Lord hears them; He delivers them from all their troubles. The Lord is close to the brokenhearted and saves those who are crushed in spirit. The righteous*

> *person may have many troubles, but the Lord delivers him from them all; He protects all his bones, not one of them will be broken.*
> *Psalm 34:17-20*

And prayer is just that—our crying out and convening with God in whatever state we find ourselves in. When I think about this, I am amazed. How can I possibly even capture the awesome privilege, blessing, magnitude, and the actual definition of prayer in words? We talk to and listen to God. We thank Him, we praise Him, we intercede for others. What fascinates (utterly amazes me) is the fact that the God of the universe, the One who created everything, is available anytime *to talk to me, an average guy!* And even when I don't know what to say, He does. Romans 8:26-27 confirms,

> *In the same way, the Spirit helps us in our weakness. We do not know what we ought to pray for, but the Spirit Himself intercedes for us through wordless groans. And He who searches our hearts knows the mind of the Spirit, because the Spirit intercedes for God's people in accordance with the will of God.*

How can that be? Even when I don't know what to pray, which seems to be often, God knows my heart and His Holy Spirit intercedes for me! And get this truth in Romans 8:24:

> *Who then is the one who condemns?*
> *No one. Christ Jesus who died—more*
> *than that, who was raised to life-is at*
> *the right hand of God and is also*
> *interceding for us.*

Jesus continues to intercede for us, on our behalf. It's beyond my comprehension. Yet sadly, I often neglect the gift of prayer, to my peril. I am grateful that I can look back at the past and recognize the tremendous value of prayer and petition. I have many journal entries that document my "calling out to God" on several occasions. Here are a few.

December 29, 2010:

While visiting family in Virginia, Dad had a medical incident in a restaurant. I planned to drive him to the Emergency Room but my wife suggested that we pray. Praise God that Dad was healed and the issue was resolved precluding a hospital visit. You are so faithful and good, Lord!

June 22, 2011:

Having health issues. Lord, if this is what it takes to draw me close to You, I'm all in. I don't want to be healed and go back to my old ways. I need You and ask that You fill me with Your Spirit and forgive me. Feeling a little better right now, thank You Lord.

January 17, 2013:

Bad day at work. Felt scolded, inadequate, and overwhelmed. Daunting task ahead today. Please give me the strength and wisdom. No idea how to figure this out.

June 2018:

Prayed for successful results of serious kidney surgery for my daughter. Also needed to find her a place to live due to immediate expiring lease.

March 13, 2020

I implore You Lord, please help us. You are our only hope and strength. Hand sanitizer, toilet paper, and stockpiles won't save us. Please stop this virus and heal us. Above all, teach us to number our days and not put our trust in anyone or anything but You.

April 19, 2020

Lord, I have let the bad news and circumstances of this world cloud my thinking. The suffering, the deaths, millions out of work. I feel guilty and helpless; I am healthy and have income. Lord, You are in control. Please help me to be empathetic and know how/where to help, but not to take on the burden of worry or guilt. You are big enough, I am not. Please give me the joy to encourage and help others. Please give our leaders and medical profession wisdom and common sense. Please take this disease from us and teach us.

God's Response and What I've Learned:

I want to share two specific responses to my journaled prayers.

On January 17, 2013, I wrote about another software issue which had brought me to my knees, literally and figuratively. I had tried everything in my analytical toolbelt to solve this complicated problem with no success. Weeks had passed and leadership was losing patience with me. When I wrote that I had no idea how to figure this out, I totally meant it; I and several others were working 24/7 to determine a solution. After crying out to God for a week and a half, I woke up the next Sunday morning and God spoke to me: "Gather a team of experts right now." I started making phone calls to trusted employees and colleagues. Thankfully, everyone showed up at the office that Sunday morning and the problem was soon solved.

And in June of 2018, my daughter came through surgery successfully. God also provided her an affordable place to live with no break in housing.

As you can see, some of these journal entries are very personal. Some requests may seem insignificant in light of bigger issues in life. But I've learned that God is interested in the intimate details of our lives and the issues which weigh us down. Be encouraged to call out to Him in all circumstances. He longs to be in fellowship with you.

I've also learned that asking for help is not a weakness. God is our ultimate Helper and Companion, but He also uses others to assist. We weren't built to shoulder heavy burdens alone. And the proof of this is my salvation. I couldn't handle the debt of my sin on my own. John 3:16 tells me that Jesus loved me enough to die for me and provide eternal life. I take this privilege for granted and treat it too much as "common." Please forgive me Lord. Please allow me to express my continual thanks in my prayers.

> *Rejoice always, pray continually, give thanks in all circumstances; for this is God's will for you in Christ Jesus.*
> *1 Thessalonians 5:17-18*

How is your prayer life? Do you "pray continually?"

How has God responded?

What changes do you need to make?

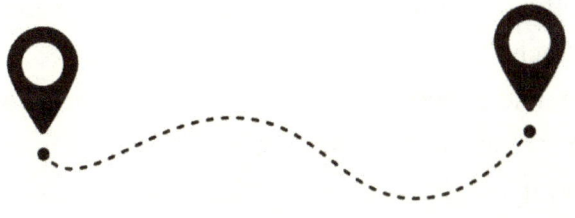

Chapter 6: The Words We Speak

The wise in heart are called discerning, and gracious words promote instruction. Prudence is a fountain of life to the prudent, but folly brings punishment to fools. The hearts of the wise make their mouths prudent, and their lips promote instruction.
Proverbs 16: 21-23

WHEN I WAS A MANAGER, EMPLOYEES WOULD OFTEN VISIT MY OFFICE to discuss a work issue or sometimes, even personal issues. I am grateful that people trusted me to provide a listening ear. One day, an employee was discussing a sensitive work issue with me, and I had the door to my office partially closed. Another employee stormed into my office and proceeded to berate me, loudly and profanely. I dismissed the employee who was sitting there, and closed my door so that the conversation with the second employee would become "private." The employee's issue was work-related and I always encouraged respectful dissent. I honestly believed that my staff were the smartest people in the office. But this was obviously more personal to him. The verbal assault was tantamount to a hand grenade being thrown at me and the tension level elevated quickly. It was the only time in my career that I ever raised my voice at someone and this was only in response to the employee yelling at me. Even though my door was closed, the "discussion" could be heard in the general office.

Like many people, I do not embrace conflict. I tried to avoid it at all costs in my career and still do, even in my marriage. Even so, my employees knew that they could come to me with any issue and I welcomed rational arguments as long as the words and tone were respectful. In this case, not only was my blood pressure amped up, I was hurt by the words and felt like I had compromised my witness. I prayed that God would forgive any bitterness in me and somehow promote reconciliation between the employee and me.

God answered my prayer beautifully and I am grateful. The next morning the employee came to my office, rendered a very sincere apology, and shook my hand. I apologized for "returning fire" and promised to consider the matter that he vehemently tried to bring to my attention. I was reminded that God is amazing and can work in the hearts of anyone, even someone like me.

The words we say can build people up or tear them down. The way that we say things also makes a difference. I've seen the impact of words from experience as an employee, a leader, a husband, a dad, and a friend. The Bible corroborates my assertion and has much to say on this topic. Here are a just a couple verses of Scripture:

> *A gentle answer turns away wrath, but a harsh word stirs up anger. The tongue of the wise adorns knowledge, but the mouth of the fool gushes folly.*
> *Proverbs 15: 1-2*

> *Let your conversation be always full of grace, seasoned with salt, so that you may know how to answer everyone.*
> *Colossians 4:6*

I am guilty to this day of sometimes speaking too soon and too much. I have also put my "foot in my mouth" far too many times to recall. Have you ever heard the expression, "shoot first, then aim?" In my zeal and desire to be "right," I've lived out this saying at times. I've observed the reality and effects of kind, encouraging words versus harsh, critical words. You can make or destroy someone's day with what you say and how you say it. I continually ask the Lord to make me slow to speak, slow to anger, and quick to listen (James 1:19).

If we profess to be followers of Jesus Christ, we need to pay attention to what we say to others and how we say it. This includes personal encounters and what we post on social media. We live in a very divided culture and it's easy to get caught up in the "noise." Depending on which "side" we are on, we can unthinkingly take a soundbite from our favorite news source, or a clever tidbit from social media, and share it as an all-encompassing truth. But often in life, issues are not simple nor black-and-white. Consequently, a simple platitude does not usually capture the entire picture.

We also often attribute intent to people and engage in ad hominem attacks without understanding every aspect of an issue. I know I am misunderstood at times, even when I have good intentions, so how *can I* possibly know what is in someone else's heart?

Years ago, I periodically encountered a man who worked in our corporate office. He had a reputation for being loud and bombastic. People would talk about him behind his back. On one occasion, he proceeded to berate me in front of several peers. His assertions were unmerited, so I took him aside privately and asked that he never disrespect me like that again. During a subsequent project, I was able to help him with a work issue, and I got to know him. He had a great deal of hurt in his past, and I believe he compensated for the pain by acting out. As I spoke words of encouragement and built a relationship with him, I discovered a hidden heart of compassion in him that most people would never get to see. I wept when I heard that he passed away several years later. He had a medical incident and died at work, much too young.

I say this to myself, and respectfully to my Christian brothers and sisters, ... I think that we can harm and even destroy our witness when we negatively engage people, even if we're on the "right" side of the issue. Think about it: Is it more important to be "right" or to be image-bearers of the One who loves and rescued us? Do you or I have perfect knowledge of someone's intent? I'm not saying that we shouldn't object to and challenge injustice, hatred, violence, false teaching, et.

al., but we should do so lovingly. Isn't that how Jesus engaged those who were against Him?

I try to ask myself the question, "Will what I'm about to say or post, even if it's true, draw someone to Christ or push them away?" I don't believe that social media is the best place for controversial topics nor heated discussions. I've seen it so many times where a brother or sister will post a statement, a trending saying, or a comment which may or may not be correct, but will likely be viewed as antagonistic. Normally those who agree will give an "Amen" and those who disagree will do so vehemently. Venting may make us temporarily feel good but the resulting comments do nothing to change anyone's mind or position. I wonder if we portray true Christianity when we interact this way.

Sometimes I'm tempted to engage when I view certain statements from all sides of the political spectrum. However, the result of my statement or retort would result in controversy, and take the focus off of Jesus Christ. Moreover, my response could be construed as the antithesis to Christian love. I find it better to have these types of discussions with individuals with whom I've built a relationship. The Bible has so much to say about our words. Here's the bottom line from 1 Peter 4:8:

Above all, love each other deeply,
because love covers over a multitude
of sins.

What matters to me is building genuine, caring relationships with people. Consequently, I believe you'll earn the right to discuss the sensitive issues.

I told you earlier about my propensity to swear when I was younger. I also had a habit of telling "dirty" jokes to get a laugh. When I became a follower of Christ, this kind of talk became offensive to me. In fact, I now view this type of language as immature since there are many other words in the English language which we can use to express ourselves. This is not meant to be a judgement but a personal observation. In the workplace, even in leadership, I am astounded at the common use of swear words in everyday speech, even among professing Christians. It doesn't compute with me, given the way we should be living. Ephesians 4:29 is very clear:

Do not let any unwholesome talk
come out of your mouths, but only
what is helpful for building others up
according to their needs, that it may
benefit those who listen.

Do I slip once in a while? I'm not going to lie, yes, especially if I get frustrated or angry about an injustice. I don't want to come across as "holier than thou" by any means, but cursing, obscene language, and coarse joking, are no longer a part of my everyday speech. This significant change has nothing to do with me though; only God could have changed that behavior in my life. Nowadays when something bad slips out, I'm immediately convicted and feel the need to repent, just like with any other sin.

Even though swearing is not part of my everyday speech, I still need help in this area. Do my words reflect the image of Jesus Christ in me? Are my words building people up or tearing them down?

I'll share a brief story from a visit to my youngest daughter's apartment in a suburb of Philadelphia. It was an innocent-enough mistake. On our way out of town, I stopped for gas at a crowded convenience store. The circular checkout counter appeared to have two lines but it was hard to discern where one began and the other ended. I walked to a cash register and had unknowingly cut into one of the lines, in front of a woman. The woman became irate and said a few choice words under her breath. I felt terrible and quickly apologized and explained that I had made a mistake. To remedy the situation, I invited her to go ahead of me. This act did not ameliorate her anger as indicated by her body language.

I silently wondered if something deeper wasn't going on in her life. In the past, I had showered people with harsh words when they cut me off or looked at me funny, so I knew it well. Yet this still seemed like an extreme reaction to an honest and admitted mistake on my part. I sensed in my spirit that I needed to engage with her. I gently said, "Ma'am, I'm really sorry, is everything okay?" When the woman realized that I was genuinely interested in her well-being, she softened and said, "I'm sorry, I've had a really bad day." I didn't want to use a platitude or cliché but wished her a better evening and told her that I would pray for her. She left the store with what appeared to be a much better attitude than I encountered when I mistakenly took her place in line.

Reflecting on other moments like these in my past, here are some selected journal entries on the topic of "Words:"

> **August 4, 2015:**
>
> My words: Is what I'm saying true, is it loving? What is my motive? Will it help anyone? Will this reflect the character of Jesus? Let my love be the highest goal.

November 26, 2016:

No "unsend" button on our speech. And God sees and hears all. Live like the "mic" is always on.

February 3, 2018:

Our words can crush someone or strengthen them.

October 23, 2019:

Weaponized words can cause scars.

God's Response and What I've Learned:

The Lord speaks to me through Psalm 19:14 which says,

> *Let the words of my mouth, and the meditation of my heart, be acceptable in Thy sight, O LORD, my Strength, and my Redeemer. (KJV)*

As an image-bearer of Christ, I need to "aim first and then shoot." Sometimes it's best that I don't "shoot" at all and remain silent. I need to carefully weigh the things I say before I say them. Words can speak life to someone or tear them down. Words are powerful things, especially those guided by the Holy Spirit.

Here is a practical lesson God taught me: No matter the situation, as a leader, a husband, a dad, et. al., I need to praise in public but criticize (constructively, thoughtfully, and lovingly) in private. I also need to speak words of encouragement to those with whom I come in contact. Who knows, I (or you), may be the only example of Jesus they see.

> *Gracious words are a honeycomb,*
> *sweet to the soul and healing to the*
> *bones.*
> *Proverbs 16:24*

Have you been on the giving or receiving end of hurtful words?

How has God responded?

What changes do you need to make?

Chapter 7: Listen Up!

My dear brothers and sisters, take note of this: Everyone should be quick to listen, slow to speak and slow to become angry.
James 1:19

AS A YOUTH, I THOROUGHLY ENJOYED PARTICIPATING IN SPORTS. My biggest sport was baseball. I started in the T-Shirt League and played all the way up until high school when I traded sports for music. I also played youth basketball and football. Sports taught me valuable lessons on teamwork and working together towards a common goal. Thinking about those experiences, I vividly remember a common phrase uttered by my coaches when they gathered the team for a talk. The coach would say,

"Listen Up!" and that was our cue that something important was about to be shared.

Boy, do I struggle with the idea of listening, even to this day.

I am guilty at times of talking too much. Moreover, sometimes when I'm in a conversation with someone I'm "half listening" and the other half of me is thinking ahead to something I want to say. There have been times in my marriage where my wife tells me something and I misunderstand because I was hearing but not really listening. There are also times when someone with expertise gives direction but I fail to follow instructions because I think I "know better." That is where my pride and desire to be "right" can trip me up. In all honesty, I sometimes do the same thing with God. Instead of seeking His wisdom and guidance, I proceed with my own plans, often with unsuccessful results. My desire for self-reliance has never paid off.

I remember a time when I was 18 or 19 years old and home for college break. A friend asked if I was interested in playing "Rat Hockey." I wasn't sure what this entailed. (Were we going to use a rat instead of a hockey puck?) Luckily, he explained that it was a pick-up game of ice hockey. The rink was part of the University in Philadelphia where the professional hockey team practiced in those days. The only available rink time was at 6 a.m. on Sunday mornings. Once I was able to borrow ice skates and the necessary equipment, off to Philly I went one fine Sunday morning.

Although I had never played ice hockey, I had some basic skating skills. I could skate forward and backwards, and was able to come to a stop when needed. I had also played street hockey as a youth and followed professional ice hockey for years, so I knew something about the sport. Because it was my first time playing though, I figured I wouldn't get any ice time. Silly thought! After my first 1+ minute shift, I couldn't wait to get off of the ice for a line change; skating up and down the frozen pond took much more energy than I imagined. I was actually on the ice more than I wanted to be. (Be careful what you ask for!)

There was a diverse mix of players on both teams. Most players were decent but a few were members of college teams and they were highly-skilled. I didn't have any speed so the team captain placed me on defense. The ability to skate backwards is a required skill in the defenseman position, so I felt like I could at least function on the ice and not embarrass myself. I enjoyed the fast-pace of the game and the players were gracious regarding my limited skills. I was happy to touch the puck at all, to not make any glaring errors, and to have all of my teeth intact at the end of the game. Interestingly, when an experienced player noticed that I was wearing a mouthpiece he chuckled and told me that the device would at least "allow me to find my teeth if I took a shot to the mouth." At the time that didn't exactly give me a comforting feeling.

At one point the opposing goalie covered the puck for a stoppage of play. This resulted in an offensive zone face off. For the face off, I was stationed at the blue line; also known as the "point." Our team captain, who played the center position, instructed me very carefully, "If I win the face off, I'll draw the puck back to you. If that happens, don't even lift your stick off of the ice, just push the puck towards the net and we'll have a chance to score." That was his plan but I had something else in mind. *(When will I ever learn?)* In pro hockey games, I had observed face offs where the defensemen would wind up and take the big slap shot. I had done it myself a hundred times in street hockey. So, my plan was to blast a 100 MPH shot to the net, contrary to the captain's instruction, and impress everyone.

Can you guess what happened? The center drew the puck back to me and I wound up for the big shot. By the time my stick came down to make contact, the puck was halfway down the ice heading the other way. You see, as a cocky young man I thought I knew better than the one who had experience. I didn't realize how fast the puck travelled along the ice. It was embarrassing!

Side note: I did redeem myself later. I found myself parked in front of the net when a teammate blasted a slap shot which the opposing goalie stopped. As the shot was coming in an opposing player knocked me down to the ice. As the goalie went down to make the save, he allowed a rebound which ended up right on my stick. I was literally on my backside but was able to lift the puck over the goalie for what was arguably the ugliest goal ever scored in the history of ice hockey. But the goal did make up for my earlier faux pas. To this day I can tell people that I scored a goal the first time I ever played ice hockey!

But seriously, can you relate to that story? Someone with experience gives you advice or guidance and you do something else because "you know better?" This experience taught me to not only listen, but to pay attention to those with wisdom. I haven't mastered this skill myself; there are still times when I fail to trust the One who has walked the road before (and beside) me. How many times do I reject what God is trying to tell me because "I know better?" Proverbs 7:24 says,

> *Now then, my sons, listen to me; pay attention to what I say.*

Listening is important to God, too. I've reflected on my journals and found some highlights on the topic of "Listening:"

> **September 12, 2015:**
>
> Most fights are about: Pride, my needing to be right, wanting my own way, ego.
>
> Wisdom says to listen and learn. Humility. Focus my eyes on You, Lord.
>
> **January 27, 2018:**
>
> Do I need to hear this (Ecclesiastes 5: 1 – 7)
>
> "Listen, do not be quick with my mouth. Do not be hasty in my heart to utter anything before God. God is in heaven. I am on earth. Let my words be few."
>
> **April 29, 2019:**
>
> Met a new friend. Shared wisdom from his experiences which helped me. I see these same stumbling blocks in myself:

1. Too high expectations for myself
2. Giving impression that I've got it all together
3. Working hard to achieve with insufficient focus on letting You work in my heart

Need to take a time of rest to listen and be still.

God's Response and What I've Learned:

While we will be measured in part by the words we speak, we also need to be good listeners. It's not always easy to develop this skill, but it's important.

I have a "Mind Game" app on my iPhone. This app tests reading, writing, math, listening, and other skills. The app accurately summarizes my skill levels which are good for reading and writing but predictably low in math (no surprise there). I also score pretty low in the skill of listening. What I find, in order to obtain a good score, is that I have to intentionally be dialed in and focused to recall what was said. God has taught me that I need to do the same with people. Just like my late grandfather "Pop" gave his full attention to me, I need to afford that same courtesy to those who I encounter. Only by listening can I get to know their joys and struggles and lift these things up to God in prayer. Attentive listening demonstrates my love for people.

When your wife, children, parents, friends, or someone you meet wants to have a conversation, put the device away, take out the earbuds, and listen up! You'll be glad you did.

What are your struggles with listening?

How has God responded?

What changes do you need to make?

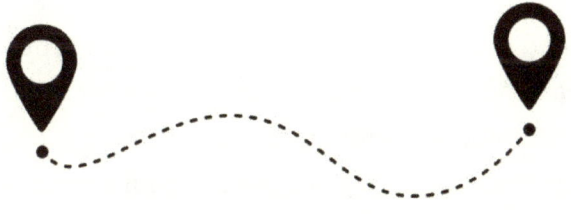

Chapter 8: A Husband, a Dad, and His Money

Whoever loves money never has enough; whoever loves wealth is never satisfied with their income. This too is meaningless.
Ecclesiastes 5:10

I ALWAYS ASSUMED THAT MY PARENTS HAD A MONEY TREE IN THE BACKYARD because we never lacked anything. If I needed money for school, it was provided. Money for sports? No problem. Music lessons? Here you go! (I never did find that tree, but it just had to be there somewhere.) The reality was that my dad worked two jobs and had the means to provide for the family. He worked twelve to fourteen hours every day to support that lifestyle.

My wife Diane, on the other hand, grew up differently. Her dad provided for everything she needed, but it was a simpler life. I think that having less gave Diane a greater appreciation for things. So much of our attitudes towards money go back to our respective childhoods.

When my wife and I first met in Texas, we were polar opposites when it came to handling money. I was a spender and she was very thrifty. She could stop on a dime (and then pick it up)! She could also stretch a dollar into a ten. She never paid full price for anything. Her parsimony served us very well early on in our marriage when our financial resources were limited.

I actually went full circle when it came to money, though. When I was in my teens, I had a paper route and worked hard for the little cash that the job provided. I was a saver and would set goals for things that I wanted to buy. After delivering papers for several years, I saved enough to buy a brand-new professional tenor saxophone. I remember how excited I was, when my dad took me to a music store in downtown Philadelphia to buy the instrument.

During my college years, I worked summers in a factory and saved every penny for tuition.

When we first got married, however, and I had a taste of significant income, I saved very little. The cost of living was high in New Jersey. I bought big-ticket items on credit and dined out quite a bit. When we needed furniture or appliances, I would use credit. When we purchased cars, I insisted on new vehicles, and that meant us taking out more loans. Diane saved her money and continued to bargain shop. My heart was in the wrong place. I was living out Ecclesiastes 5:10; I loved making money, I pursued it, and always worried that I wouldn't have enough. This may explain why I was consumed with work as a husband and father; subconsciously I was afraid of losing my job and not having the means to support my family. We lived simply, but I still spent money I didn't have. Often, we'd run out of money before we ran out of month. God always provided for our needs, but I failed to manage money with the proper heart and motives.

When I gave my life to Jesus Christ, we had been married for about seven years. I read my Bible and began to understand what God had to say about money. I'd heard well-meaning people say that the Bible teaches that money is the root of all evil. When I studied the Bible though, I learned that was inaccurate. That "saying" is a variation on 1 Timothy 6:10 which actually states,

> *For the love of money is a root of all kinds of evil. Some people, eager for money, have wandered from the faith and pierced themselves with many griefs.*

The issue wasn't with money itself; it was my attitude towards it—the "love of money." I realized that the Bible was saying that there is nothing wrong with having money; we need it to survive. But it is only a tool. When we become obsessed with making money or make it an idol, that's where we get into trouble. I speak from experience.

Jesus had so much to say about money and it all boils down to our hearts and perspective. Matthew 6:24 says,

> *No one can serve two masters. Either you will hate the one and love the other, or you will be devoted to the one and despise the other. You cannot serve both God and money.*

Did you catch that? As with everything else in life, we are to put God first. Money is a valuable commodity but the pursuit of/obsession with it, can become an idol. And like any idol, it takes the place of God in your life, yet you cannot depend on it for security. The Lord Jesus Christ is our only hope and we need to place our complete trust in Him. He has always been faithful!

Once I learned God's perspective on money, I knew that it was time for my perspective to change. I read a few books and listened to radio broadcasts by Christians who provided Biblical insight about money. I came to understand that it was God who provided for me through the abilities He allowed me to have. Deuteronomy 8:18 says:

> *But remember the LORD your God,*
> *for it is He who gives you the ability*
> *to produce wealth, and so confirms*
> *His covenant, which He swore to your*
> *ancestors, as it is today.*

Another great verse comes from Ecclesiastes 2:24-25:

> *A person can do nothing better than*
> *to eat and drink and find satisfaction*
> *in their own toil. This too, I see, is*
> *from the hand of God, for without*
> *Him, who can eat or find enjoyment?*

I began to understand that money, like everything else, belongs to God. In fact, everything I have, is only because He provided it. Therefore, if God gave me the ability to make money, i.e., my job, it belongs to Him, and I am a steward (a manager of God's money), *not an owner*. It's not that I can't use money for enjoyable things, but I need to manage it with the proper perspective. Part of that involves giving back to God's work.

Fast forward to 2020, and I've become Diane. I watch what we spend and put aside money for real estate taxes, insurance, etc. She still hunts for bargains but comes home with a load of goods based on a big sale at the local department store. I'll roll my eyes at the plethora of merchandise and she'll say, "But I saved $50!" I'll reply, tongue in cheek of course, "You save $50 every other day!" The wonderful thing is that Diane also shares my heart to be generous to those in need.

As we've journeyed together with Him, we've witnessed God's hand on our finances so many times. When my middle daughter was in her senior year of an expensive private college (fortunately a scholarship defrayed some of the cost), she called and gleefully informed us that she had been accepted to a Master's program at a college outside of Philadelphia. "Isn't that great?" she exclaimed. While I was happy for her, I knew that she did not have the money for tuition, nor living expenses (apartment, car, fuel, food, etc.). I had no idea how we would swing it and wondered if we would have to say "no" to this opportunity. God, however, orchestrated miraculous events by raising up a roommate to share expenses and a Grad Assistant position which took care of tuition. We were still stretched financially, but God made a way when it looked like it was a dead end. There were times, especially early on, where I wasn't sure how we would pay for something without using credit. That's where God miraculously provided. He is faithful!

Through the years, there have been many journal entries regarding my concerns over money. For the purpose of this book, I've selected just a few journal entries here.

May 6, 2000:

I am concerned about our finances. This week I am short for my tithe and have nothing left for the week. Will need to borrow from here and there. Then there is kids' camp, gymnastics, piano lessons, and a car repair to pay for. Please help us to meet our needs, Lord.

May 24, 2014:

Father, I know that folks have much more difficult issues but I'm asking for wisdom with our finances. Please help me to make right decisions.

May 24, 2015:

Really anxious about finances. Our daughter in college needs $750 a month for rent, due next week. How will I swing it? Will I be able to retire when planned? Then I read in Isaiah 41:10 "Fear not, for I am with You. Be not dismayed, for I am your God. I will strengthen you and help you; I will uphold you with My righteous right hand."

God's Response and What I've Learned:

Lest you think that I have it all figured out, think again. In spite of my best intentions and plans, unexpected things have happened and continue to happen. At the beginning of our marriage, I had credit card debt, a huge mortgage, and a large car payment. I had to reduce the debt before I could earnestly save for the future. A good lesson for me was that if I did add a charge to my credit card, that I had to be self-disciplined and commit to pay it off at the end of the month.

Over the years, I've experienced all of the following concerns and more.

- Purchasing/maintaining a home
- Paying a mortgage

- Putting three kids through college
- Significant debt
- Potential loss of income due to downsizing
- Transmission failure
- Roof replacement

Amazingly, God has always provided for us—often not in the way I desired or expected.

This is not a financial book, but I'll summarize what the Lord taught me in the process. I realized if I was going to manage our resources well, I needed to have a budget each month as a spending plan. Practically speaking, I found this to be a critical tool to manage what God had so graciously provided. As a plan for the distribution of our income, I learned not to get discouraged when I had to adjust the budget, as circumstances changed.

There are many books and resources on how to create a budget, but I chose to use a simple spreadsheet. In a nutshell, I listed my income for the month and subtracted out:

- Giving to my church and other charities God placed on my heart
- Emergency Savings (The first thing I did was establish a $1000 Emergency Fund for unforeseen expenses, e.g., major car repair.

If you're not in a position, as I wasn't at first, to save $1000, start somewhere and save what you can.)
- Long-term savings (This means different things to different people depending on where you are in life. This category could include college savings for kids, vacations, retirement, etc.)
- Monthly bills/expenses, listed individually (e.g., electric, fuel, etc.)
- Quarterly/annual expenses
- I also include categories for gifts, dining out, vacations, etc.

With simple addition and subtraction, I ensured that the plan allowed me to allocate all of the resources to a category. I am not a financial expert, so I'll stop there, and simply state that a budget has been a good tool to manage the money that God has provided. (The budget should obviously be tailored to your specific financial situation. If you've never formulated and used a budget, I would highly recommend you consider one.)

I'm grateful that Diane and I have become complimentary to one another in our ideas of handling money. That's been a learning process too, but an important one. Disagreements about money can cause issues in marriage, not to mention health issues.

Here are some principles I've discovered for my own marriage:

1. Be generous because God has been so good to me.
2. It is not "my money," but rather "our money." And my wife is free to have her own spending money to use as she pleases.
3. Be transparent about our income and budget. Determine who will keep the budget and pay the bills. I have this responsibility in my home, not because I demand it, but because my wife prefers it that way. I keep her apprised of everything.
4. Discuss big purchases and decide together.

For years I pursued wealth under the guise of ambition. God has taught me to not run after wealth, but to be content with what I have. Above all, He has taught me to be generous because He has lavished so much upon me. He gave me everything I have and I find great joy in giving to those in need. 1 Timothy 6:6 says,

But godliness with contentment is great gain.

One final thing: God gave us all things to enjoy, and that includes our financial resources. The key to all of this, is keeping money in its proper perspective. 1 Timothy 6:17 captures this principle very well:

> *Command those who are rich in this present world not to be arrogant nor to put their hope in wealth, which is so uncertain, but to put their hope in God, who richly provides us with everything for our enjoyment.*

What are your money issues?

How has God responded?

What changes do you need to make?

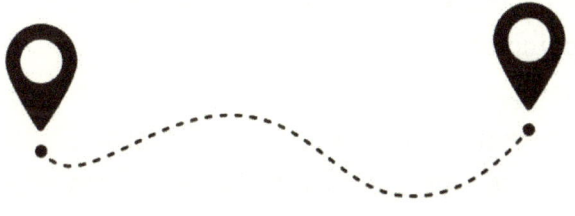

Chapter 9: Making the Most of Opportunities

*Be very careful, then, how you live—
not as unwise but as wise, making
the most of every opportunity,
because the days are evil.
Ephesians 5:15-16*

ONE OF OUR SUNDAY SCHOOL CLASS MEMBERS COLLECTED A NUMBER OF NICE CLOTH SHOPPING BAGS, and filled them with some basic provisions, including water, snacks, and packs of tissues. She made these "blessing bags" available to assist the less fortunate in our community. My wife and I kept a couple of bags in the trunk of the car, not knowing if, or how, we'd ever distribute any.

One evening, my wife and I went out to dinner at a semi-expensive restaurant which was situated in a shopping center. As we pulled into the plaza, we noticed a couple with their child standing beside the access road to the parking lot. The husband held up a sign which indicated that the family needed help. I thought to myself, *this is a great opportunity to give away one of the bags!* I stopped the car, rolled down the window, and handed a bag to the man and proceeded to the restaurant. I felt good about my act of service.

As we enjoyed dinner, I was convicted that I simply handed a bag to the family we encountered. I did not get to know anything about them and what their needs were. Moreover, I had spent a sum on dinner which could have really helped a needy family. The "blessing bag" cost me nothing. I prayed that the Lord would forgive me, and provide another opportunity to interact with this family.

As we left the plaza, I saw that the family was still there and I got out of the car and spoke with the father. It was clear that this family was new to our country and he explained that his car needed a part that he couldn't afford. He required the vehicle to get to work. It was also clear that this family had very little. The man showed me the paperwork for the car and I sensed in my heart that he and his family had legitimate needs. I was grateful to give to them although it was little in comparison to how the Lord has provided to my family.

I'm convinced that our service needs to cost us something, whether it's time, attention, financial resources, or whatever God asks of us. The wonderful thing is that He blesses us when we bless others. When you consider the world population and the average income, we are extremely blessed in the United States. I was grateful for the opportunity to show God's blessings to this family.

As I reflect on my life, I cannot count the number of times the Lord has brought wonderful strangers across my path. Each time I travelled for business, I asked God for ways to show Jesus to others, even if my actions seemed insignificant. Opening a door, offering to help someone place a heavy carry-on in an airplane's overhead compartment, giving a smile to someone who needed it, stopping with a homeless person to hear their story; these were all opportunities. God has opened up many opportunities when I've sought ways to bless others. I've encountered people in airports, on flights, in the workplace, and throughout our society. In every case I have been extremely blessed and I pray that I was a blessing to them. A number of those encounters even resulted in long-term friendships.

One example of this, was a new friendship with a lady named Anna, who provided an example to me of making the most of an opportunity with a "stranger."

Anna

In the late 1990s I was on a two-week business trip to a small town in Germany. Between high school and college, I had studied the language for a total of eight years. However, so much time had passed that my German was rusty. When I arrived at the hotel in a small German town, it became clear that I would need to dust off the cobwebs in my brain. The hotel receptionist did not speak English, so I did my best to communicate and complete the check-in process.

On Sunday morning of the first week, I sat down in the hotel dining area for a typical German breakfast, which consisted of delicious breads, meats, cheeses, and coffee. I was alone at a table with four place settings. An elderly woman with coffee in hand approached my table. She spoke no English and asked me several questions in German. I had to answer each one individually: "Is anyone using this plate? Is anyone using this silverware? Is anyone sitting here?" After politely responding, "Nein," to each question, I finally invited her to sit down and join me.

Her name was "Anna" and it mattered not to her that I struggled to remember proper German sentence structure and vocabulary. If I didn't understand something, I let her know, and she said it another way. Nothing would deter her from having a conversation. She spoke to me as if we'd known each other all of our lives. What started out as an awkward moment for me became a very comfortable, friendly encounter. It also kept my brain cells firing as I had to think hard to recall German words and expressions.

Over the next week, before I left for work each morning, Anna would join me at breakfast. I learned about her family and the fascinating history of the town we were in. One morning, she handed me a book, autographed by a past leader in that city. I told her that I would look it over and get the book back to her before I left Germany. She said, "No, I want you to have it."

On the final morning, before I left for Frankfurt to fly home, Anna thanked me for being a friend and a blessing to her. She had no idea how much of a blessing she was to me. I told her that I took no credit for anything good in me; I gave all glory to Jesus. We exchanged addresses and promised to write to each other.

Anna and I kept in touch for a while. The first Christmas after that trip, I received a letter from her along with two German books. One was a novel for me, and the other a children's book for my kids. (To be honest, the children's book was more readable for me given the years that had passed.) I understood from one of the hotel staff that Anna's health was not good, which likely explains why I stopped receiving letters after a few years. She was a sweet, down-to-earth friend who crossed my path one morning in Germany. I am so grateful that she stopped at my table that Sunday morning. I believe that God ordained that meeting. Not only did Anna reawaken my love for the German language, but she also blessed me beyond belief.

Looking back, all of the business trips I made, had their significance in terms of my job and responsibilities. But God was working in a much bigger way; there was a reason that I was where I was at those moments in time. Remember the "Upper Story" I mentioned earlier? Do I know the purpose of what God was up to in these precious moments? Not exactly, but I do know that He brought me great blessing through others, even when I had to be away from my family. I also have a feeling that there will be a great reunion someday in heaven! I can't wait to hear the full upper stories.

It is so important we make the most out of the opportunities we are afforded. The world is watching what we say and how we live. If I had dismissed Anna, I would have missed out on the blessing of an unexpected friendship. If I had missed seeing that family once more outside the restaurant, I would have left them with a rather shallow witness that cost me nothing. I don't want to say one thing and live another way. I believe that I was "saved to serve" and I want my heart to reflect that.

> **From my journal June 29, 2018:**
>
> Am I loving?
>
> Am I serving?
>
> Am I giving?
>
> Is it costing me something?

God's Response and What I've Learned:

In everything I do, I believe that God has called me to love and serve others. The Bible indicates that He has called all of us who follow Jesus to do the same. We can do this in so many simple ways, just through a kind word or act. Not only does a heart of service bless others but it blesses us as well.

These two verses are profound:

> *In everything I did, I showed you that by this kind of hard work we must help the weak, remembering the words the LORD Jesus himself said: "It is more blessed to give than to receive."*
> *Acts 20:35*

> *But King David replied to Araunah, "No, I insist on paying the full price. I will not take for the LORD what is yours, or sacrifice a burnt offering that costs me nothing."*
> *1 Chronicles 21:24*

In his book, *Biking Across America*, author Paul Stutzman says this:

> You may be the person who can make a difference in someone else's life. The next time you are having a frustrating day and it seems that nothing is falling into place, be patient and watchful; a divine encounter may be just around the corner.[1]

---

[1] Paul Stutzman, *Biking Across America: My Coast-To-Coast Adventure and the People I Met Along the Way* (Grand Rapids: Revell, 2013).

In my journey, I've found that my Companion uses individual encounters and relationships to bless people and change lives.

> *Be wise in the way you act toward outsiders; make the most of every opportunity.*
> *Colossians 4:5*

Are there areas in your life where you can serve and bless others?

How has God responded?

What changes do you need to make?

Chapter 10: Loving Difficult People

If it is possible, as far as it depends on you, live at peace with everyone.
Romans 12:18

WHILE WAITING TO DEPLANE IN THE SINGLE FILE SEA OF HUMANITY, I FELT SOMETHING POKING ME IN THE BACK. At first, I assumed that someone had accidentally bumped me. However, when the poking and pushing continued, I surmised that it was intentional. I turned my head to notice a lady, maybe five feet tall, who was attempting to get past me. I politely said, "Ma'am, there is only one way off of this plane and it's a single file, narrow aisle. I can only move as quickly as the person in front of me." She kept pushing and repeating, "I have flight to catch." After a long delay in Seattle and an even longer flight to D.C., I sarcastically responded, "Don't we all." Undeterred by my response, she continued to push and poke. I know that the Holy Spirit was working in me because He kept my desired response in check. I finally ducked into the nearest seat, turned to the lady, and said, "Be my guest." She proceeded to move forward and poke the next person in line. He was not as "kind" as I had been.

The reality was, everyone on the plane had somewhere to be. And since this airport was a large connection hub, I suspect that most travelers had missed their subsequent flight due to the long delay we had experienced in taking off from Seattle.

It was early in 2008, and this particular trip was at the end of a week-long work assignment which had taken a lot out of me. I had been in charge of an intense project and had worked long hours that week. I was anxious to get home to my family. My route that day consisted of a long cross-country flight from Seattle to Washington, D.C., and then a short connecting flight to Harrisburg, Pennsylvania. When I had scheduled the flights, there was originally a significant amount of layover time in D.C. so, I figured that even if we were delayed in Seattle, I would still make the connecting flight home. At least, that was until the four-hour delay in Seattle. After 9/11, I'd become accustomed to delays and cancellations and tried to exercise patience. In this case, I wasn't sure what I would do once I arrived in Washington, but it would be good just to be back on the East Coast. I tried to settle into my usual routine of sipping coffee, reading, and listening to music as I waited to board the plane.

At first the delay was anticipated to be a short one, so it did not phase me given the scheduled layover time in D.C. However, as time went on, one hour became two, and then three. Eventually, I wondered if the flight would be cancelled. I'd seen this situation too often. I can't tell you how many times over my career that I've been delayed, diverted to cities I'd never been to, and stuck overnight in an airport. I always tried to roll with the punches, but return flights were tough due to my desire to get home after a long trip.

When our flight arrived in Washington, D.C., it was after 9 p.m. and that's when I was getting poked in the back. I knew by the time I deplaned, the connecting flight to Harrisburg would be long gone, and I would have decisions to make about how to continue my journey home. I was tired and my patience was thinner than usual, as I'm sure was the case for every passenger on the flight. We were all in the same boat.

Once I got to the terminal, I considered a rental car, but by the time I would have rented a car and driven to Harrisburg, I would have arrived slightly earlier than a flight that the airline was offering to book me for, on the next morning. I was tired, so I opted to sleep for a few hours at a local hotel. But before that could happen, myself and my colleague waited over an hour, in the cold, for a hotel shuttle that never came. Finally, a shuttle driver from a different hotel, who had seen us several times on his repeated trips to the airport, took pity on us. He offered us rooms at his hotel. I was so tired that I accepted that invitation. I got home early the next morning which was a blessing. Better late than never! It was a long trip.

As far as the young lady who felt that she was the most important person on the flight, my heart did go out to her. I assume from her use of the English language that the U.S. was not her original homeland. In my state of mind, I tried to show her compassion even though her efforts to get ahead of everyone in line were futile.

Truthfully, we never know what a person is going through, if they are fearful, what their history is, or anything else about them. God has shown me nothing but grace and I need to offer the same to those around me. I have not perfected the quality of empathy, but I continue to work on it. I am a flawed human being and need God's help moment by moment. I'm glad He was on the journey with me that day! One thing I've learned: When we put others' needs before ours, there is great blessing. Philippians 2:3 reminds me,

> *Do nothing out of selfish ambition or vain conceit. Rather, in humility value others above yourselves ...*

Yet even with this wisdom from Scripture, I don't enjoy being around people who are continually negative or specialize in giving me a hard time. We've all experienced the "joy" of being in the company of people who seemingly live to argue, complain, or just upset the proverbial "apple cart." If you state that the sky is blue, they'll argue that it's green. I could fill a book with stories about difficult people I've encountered in the workplace, in society, and even in church! However, if I'm honest, I can also be a difficult person at times.

Before I became a disciple of Jesus Christ, I had a cynical and negative side which could rub people the wrong way. I'd like to say that I've completely overcome this, but old habits die hard; that personality trait still rears its ugly head at times. I must confess that I sometimes get upset with drivers who tailgate, cut me off, or speed dangerously. My ultimate pet peeve is with drivers who have eyes glued to their cell phones, or even text while driving. It irritates me because I feel like they are jeopardizing my life and that of my loved ones with their behavior. I have never gotten to the point where I've yelled or made eye contact, but I'll silently condemn them in my mind. Truth be told, I have no idea if the person is having a bad day, just made a mistake, is on their way to the hospital, or just has no self-awareness. Perhaps they think that what they're doing is fine, similar to my way of thinking when I was younger. And really, do I seriously think that I never make a mistake on the road and am the world's best driver? My wife often has to often tell me to "calm down," and her reminders have helped me to overlook others' poor driving habits.

Over the years I've also struggled at times with severe headaches, sometimes for weeks and months. For those of you who suffer from migraines, you know how debilitating they can be. They can affect your mood and ability to function. During these times, it's a struggle for me to be around other people. I can be difficult and short with people when I don't feel well. I praise God that He has been there to comfort and strengthen me. Sometimes the headache doesn't subside right away, but His presence and peace see me through the times when I do not have the motivation to press on.

Here is a journal entry which summarizes how I can react when it comes to difficult people. Thank God that He spoke through my daughter when this happened:

> **December 23, 2015: 6 p.m.**
>
> Tonight, my youngest daughter kept me from being a person I didn't want to be. I had my turn signal on to take a space in a very crowded parking lot. A guy pulled in, right in front of me, and took the spot. I rolled my window down to say something and my daughter spoke up and helped me to keep my head. I let it go, and it was the right thing to do. I do tend to get annoyed with drivers who speed, text while driving, don't use signals, and drive aggressively. At times I want to give a dirty look or somehow express my displeasure. First, they would be ungodly responses. Second, practically, the outcome would never be good. I wish that people would be more courteous and safer on the roads, but I've seen evidence of road rage in my many years of driving. Never a good outcome for anyone.

God's Response and What I've Learned:

God has taught me that it takes a daily intentional effort to look inwardly before looking at others. I don't know what someone is going through. It is so easy to look at the faults of others and miss my own shortcomings. Matthew 7:5 says,

> *You hypocrite, first take the plank out of your own eye, and then you will see clearly to remove the speck from your brother's eye.*

Most importantly, everything I do, regardless of the person, needs to be covered in love. Jesus died for me even when I was ungodly. I rely on two important verses as a reminder to deal with difficult people in love:

> *Whoever claims to love God yet hates a brother or sister is a liar. For whoever does not love their brother and sister, whom they have seen, cannot love God, whom they have not seen.*
> *1 John 4:20*

> *Above all, love each other deeply, because love covers over a multitude of sins.*
> *1 Peter 4:8*

What are your struggles with difficult people?

When have you been a difficult person, and how has God responded?

What changes do you need to make?

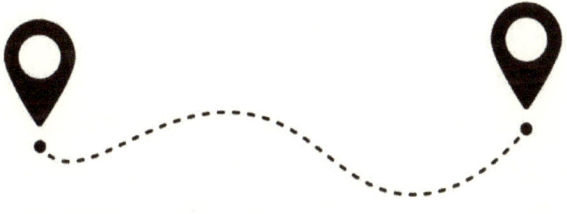

Chapter 11: My Struggles with "Self"

For by the grace given me I say to every one of you: Do not think of yourself more highly than you ought, but rather think of yourself with sober judgment, in accordance with the faith God has distributed to each of you.
Romans 12:3

IN THE SUMMER OF 2013, AN ANOMALY WAS FOUND DURING WHAT WE EXPECTED TO BE A ROUTINE MAMMOGRAM FOR MY WIFE. Diane was told that the cyst could be benign, but could also be something worse. The procedure was scheduled for September

3rd. Diane did not make a big deal about the appointment and honestly, I hadn't given it much thought. It was a busy time at work (in reality, I was always "busy"), so the thought never occurred to me that I should accompany her to the appointment. I didn't realize at the time that my wife was apprehensive, if not downright scared, about what the procedure might reveal. How could I have been so blind? Check out my journal entry …

> **September 1, 2013:**
>
> Praying for Diane's procedure this week. May there be no pain and nothing wrong. Thank You Lord!

Gee, what a great token prayer for my wife. Little did I know how powerfully God would answer, in spite of my self-absorption.

The next day was Labor Day. During my quiet time, once again (thankfully), the Holy Spirit spoke to my heart. I don't remember exactly what the Lord told me but, I deserved something like, "What could you possibly be thinking, you need to be there for your wife! How could you let work come before this?" I was grateful that my Almighty Companion clued me in.

On September 3, Diane had the procedure and I accompanied her. When the technician inserted the probe to biopsy the "cyst," it miraculously disappeared as the instrument touched the area displayed on the screen. The technician was amazed, and we considered this to be a genuine miracle. I was, and am, so grateful for the miraculous results. I asked for Diane's forgiveness, even though she felt no anger towards me for my initially selfish decision. Once again, I proved that I am not the brightest bulb in the box, and am still learning. Sometimes it takes me awhile, but I serve an almighty, amazing, loving, gracious, merciful, sovereign God who has gone with me all the way, even as I have tripped on "self."

I want to be very transparent about two extremes which have been a personal struggle for me, even as a believer: self-centeredness and self-esteem.

Self-Centeredness

Have you ever heard this statement? "If it's to be, it's because of me."

I've heard this said both in the Christian and secular worlds. I understand the sentiment; God gave us abilities and we need to have initiative and be responsible for tasks. But statements like this can also promote self-reliance and pride. I don't know if it is said these days but, years ago, this little quote also made the rounds: "So and so is a self-made man." Hmm ... I'm a literal person, so I find a little humor in that statement. A self-created person would be something to behold! Seriously, people would attribute this expression to someone who worked their way up to a successful position, seemingly without anyone's help. I used to live with the same attitude! I've learned a lot about the concept of "self" thanks be to my Companion who has been gracious to sustain me through the lessons.

One thing I've learned is that the Bible takes an opposite view of self from that previous concept. Jesus says to "deny self" and that apart from Him, we can do nothing (Matt 16:24, Luke 9:23, Mark 8:34, Luke 14:27, John 15:5). The Apostle Paul reminds us that we should consider others better than ourselves. Philippians 2:3 says,

> *Do nothing out of selfish ambition or vain conceit. Rather, in humility value others above yourselves.*

These principles are totally counter to the world today where almost everything is focused on self-gratification. And they are totally counter to how I lived before I became a believer! Focusing on self might be our instinctual reaction, but believers are meant to put their focus on God instead. Jesus, quoting from the Old Testament, said this in Mark 12:30-31:

> *Love the Lord your God with all your heart and with all your soul and with all your mind and with all your strength. The second is this: Love your neighbor as yourself. There is no commandment greater than these.*

Many people will falsely misinterpret this verse to mean that Jesus is telling us to "love ourselves." No, Jesus is telling us to love our neighbors as *we already* love ourselves. See, "loving" or focusing on ourselves is something we do from the moment we're born. It's instinctual in us because of our sin nature. "Dying to self" and "denying self" as Jesus instructs, takes a focus off of self and instead places it on loving God first, and others second. When we put God first and others second, and do not act in selfish ways, it's amazing how our life purpose and significance fall into place. We will find joy in our work, our families, and aspects of life that we never noticed before. But it's tough; it means that we relinquish control and self-reliance in favor of dependence on an Almighty God. This truth was one of the most difficult for me to embrace when I first surrendered my life to Jesus standing by the New Jersey Turnpike. I was used to controlling everything, even though in reality, I did not have control.

So, great, Bob, you have it all together *now*, right? Not at all. Then the question remains, if I'm a believer, and I understand these biblical principles, why do I still struggle with self-centeredness? I believe that the Apostle Paul captured my conundrum perfectly in Romans 7: 21- 25:

> *So I find this law at work: Although I want to do good, evil is right there with me. For in my inner being I delight in God's law; but I see another law at work in me, waging war against the law of my mind and making me a prisoner of the law of sin at work within me. What a wretched man I am! Who will rescue me from this body that is subject to death? Thanks be to God, who delivers me through Jesus Christ our Lord! So then, I myself in my mind am a slave to God's law, but in my sinful nature a slave to the law of sin.*

Did you catch the conclusion in that last verse: "Thanks be to God, who delivers me through Jesus Christ our Lord!" You see, until we leave this earth and shed these bodies, with their sinful nature, we will all struggle with "self" at times. Here is what I have found: As a follower of Jesus Christ, and one who has been mercifully rescued from sin, I know that the Holy Spirit lives in me because He makes me uncomfortable being comfortable. As you'll see from the stories below, when I look to my own desires and wanting things my own way, I end up under great conviction. I am so grateful for my Almighty Companion's patience with me as we journey along. He shows me that He is interested in the most intimate details of my life.

Can I Ask You a Favor?

Whenever I fly, I select an aisle seat ahead of time, especially for long flights. I like the elbow room, but, more than that, I enjoy the convenience of slipping out to the restroom. I don't like disrupting passengers when I need to go, but I don't mind getting up for them. I plan ahead, but sometimes still end up in a middle or window seat. Now, if I fly with my wife, all bets are off; she loves the window seat so I accommodate her and sit in the middle seat.

In 2018, I was on the second leg of a business trip to the San Francisco area, and had just boarded a plane in Philadelphia. A nice young lady showed up at my row and it was clear that she was assigned the middle seat next to me. Her fiancé was seated in the middle seat of the previous row. I was settled in, and the lady politely asked if I could switch seats with her fiancé so that they could sit together. I remember her voice like it was yesterday: "You can say no, but can I ask you a favor? Would you be willing to sit there so that my fiancé and I could sit together?" My thoughts immediately went to my own needs, the length of the flight, and my own comfort. I politely replied, "I wish I could, but I really prefer the aisle seat." What a witness, huh? Almost immediately, I was under tremendous conviction, but it seemed awkward to reverse my position once the doors to the plane were closed.

Providentially, our flight was delayed due to mechanical issues. We sat on the plane for an hour and were ultimately directed to deplane. Mechanics tried to make repairs, but eventually a new plane was brought in. The entire process took hours, and my plans to arrive in San Francisco before rush hour were scuttled. When we boarded the replacement plane, I sat in the middle seat of the row in front of my assigned seat. When the couple subsequently boarded, they noticed my gesture and expressed gratitude. I apologized for my original selfishness and was grateful that God gave me the opportunity to eventually show the love of Jesus to the couple. I still feel like I blew it because my obedience wasn't immediate, but God is in the business of redemption, even when we fail. I am so grateful for His grace and patience.

The Shoe Shine

At the conclusion of a business trip in the St. Louis area, I was walking to my airport gate located at the end of a terminal. I passed several gates and heard this voice say, "Shine 'em up for you, Sir?" I turned my head to notice a gentleman whose profession was shoe-shining. In typical fashion, without breaking stride, I said "No, thank you" and kept walking. First, I didn't want to spend the money for a shoe shine. Second, I was wearing an old pair of casual shoes which didn't really lend themselves to a polish. Third, I didn't want to give the impression that I was some rich guy who needed to have someone shine his shoes. I'd never had a shoe shine in my life. That seemed like a luxury as opposed to a "need."

As I continued my journey to the gate, I heard that still, small voice which said: "Bob, you need to go back." Here was a hardworking man, charging $5 to shine a pair of shoes. Surely, I could afford that, and perhaps bless this man. My Almighty Companion was directing me that this had nothing to do with a shoe shine but more with a relationship. *When will I ever learn?*

I went back. The gentleman's name was Willy and I was blessed to talk with him. I learned that he lived in St. Louis all his life, was never married, and knew everything about the city. He had so much life experience, and I listened intently to his interesting stories. I asked lots of questions which he graciously answered. Somehow, he was able to make a living for 26 years shining shoes. That fact astounded me! He was obviously also a man of high moral standards and integrity. We talked about Jesus, which was a blessing to me. He spent a great deal of time at his work and was meticulous with his skills. Amazingly, my shoes had never looked better when he was finished with the job. The shoeshine was worth so much more than $5. I knew that God had ordained that moment in time and I made sure that I compensated Willy for the great work. As I walked away, he told me that I had made his day. In reality, he made mine.

Self-Esteem

If you ask most of my friends or former colleagues, they would likely tell you that I am an upbeat, positive, joyful person. And because of Jesus Christ in my life, that is generally a true statement. But battles are fought in my mind, and, deep down, I continually question if I'm good enough, smart enough, and doing enough. It seems hard to believe that a guy like me who is sometimes self-centered, would also struggle with self-esteem issues. But it's true. What I've learned is that a focus on self usually lends to both of these traits, (self-centeredness and low self-esteem), and we are sometimes more fooled into a focus on self by means of inappropriate condemnation of ourselves. When we claim a low self-esteem, it's really just another way for the enemy to keep us focused on ourselves and pursue self-reliance. There is a fine line between understanding who we are in Christ because He is our Almighty Companion, and also understanding that we can do nothing without Him.

As I noted before, music has been an important part of my life for many reasons. Aside from journal entries, I have also enjoyed some song writing which has expressed, and helped me to process some of my own struggles. In one example, I wrote a song called, "My Own Worst Enemy." The lyrics originated from the honest perspective that no one is harder on me, than me. The lyrics reflect my battle with self-condemnation:

> I have made mistakes, and I have done some things I regret. And I play those "old tapes" that tell me I'm not good enough. Could it be, I'm my own worst enemy? I have everything I need, but I choose to be defined by the thoughts in my head. Is there any hope for me?

> Will I ever feel the peace? Can I ever be free from my own worst enemy?

Much of my struggle goes back to childhood where I first began accepting and claiming various "labels." Whether it was intentional or unintentional, my parents, teachers, adults, and other kids applied labels to me. If I'm totally honest, I have also labelled others myself, both in my mind and verbally. Labels are nothing new, of course. In fact, I think that technology and social media make it much easier today to "label" people. Labels, like words, can build people up or tear them down.

It still stings when I think about the "labels" that I believed applied to me growing up. It also hurts to think about the people I secretly or verbally labelled. I was "stupid" because I struggled with high school algebra. I was "ugly" because of acne. I was a "nerd" because of the way I dressed or the friends I kept. I was "unimportant" because my parents seldom came to my sporting events due to work or other responsibilities. I was also "inadequate" when compared with other people. Sometimes good labels were stamped on me, such as, "job well done" or "I'm proud of you." But the negative labels stuck to me like glue.

As an adult I have been self-conscious of many things, including my appearance, weight, musical, and professional abilities. I was obsessed with being the best (a perfectionist), so that I wasn't found out for my true self, which I perceived as "stupid." See how those old tapes can play in our heads? At times, I have failed to ask God and others for help for fear of comments such as, "you should have known that," or "how did you ever become a boss," or "you call yourself a musician?" The reality is that most people probably do not think of me, in the way I believe they do. Yet, self-esteem issues would have me so focused on myself, that I believe they are as well!

My wife knows me better than anyone. After teaching a class or doing a music gig, I'll question how I did and seek approval of my "performance." I'll be quick to ask her, "How do you think Sunday School went? Did I talk too much? Did my voice sound okay when I sang?" This way of thinking boils down to "self" and my obsession with what others think. It's sinful because the focus on self takes my eyes off of Jesus. The truth is, it doesn't really matter what others think of me. It's about what God thinks.

During my career, especially early on, I found my identity and my significance in my job. I am not an expert in psychology or human behavior, so I don't know if this is primarily an issue for men, or if it applies to everyone. I think that deep down most people want significance, that is, knowing that we are here for a purpose. We need a reason to get out of bed in the morning, and also want to be noticed.

Work does have its place, but it shouldn't be first in our lives. I learned this the hard way. There is a balance between being conscientious and making time for others. I wore my career like a badge and felt like my value and security were tied to what I did for a living. I put work in front of family (as you read in the first story), and I seldom took time off for fear of missing out on something at work. I also wanted to appear to be dedicated and not lazy, stupid, or incompetent. It was as if I had to keep earning the right to be in my position. I knew so little about the grace of God, and my identity in Jesus Christ. I also failed to realize that my career, my health, and things I relied on for stability, could all be taken away in an instant.

As I've grown older, God has taught me to be less self-reliant, and more dependent upon Him. Perfectionism is ingrained in my nature and it caused significant stress and health issues over the years. The need to be perfect, the need for approval, and obsession with "what others think of me," have taken their toll. The truth is that no one is perfect, except for Jesus Christ. All of us will fail at times but that does not make us "failures." I don't need to wear that label. And I've learned that the greatest lessons in life, often come from our failures.

Don't get me wrong; I've seen the opposite of low self-esteem in the form of pride. This too, is another form of self-focus. I know plenty of people who are overly comfortable in their own skin and won't hesitate to boast about their qualifications and abilities at every opportunity. In fact, I've been guilty of self-promotion at times to overcompensate for feelings of inadequacy and the need for approval. But I try to err on the side of empathy and attempt to understand that there may be more going on in a person's life than I can see.

Here is something I've learned as a result of following Jesus. Low self-esteem and inordinately high self-esteem are both sinful. Both extremes take our eyes off of Jesus and place the focus on ourselves. When we have low self-esteem, we desecrate the value that God has placed upon us. He loves and values each of us so much that He sent His Son to die for us. On the other hand, when we think too highly of ourselves, we can become arrogant and self-righteous. This results in pride which is a well-covered topic in the Bible. In fact, 1 Peter 5:5 says,

> *All of you, clothe yourselves with humility toward one another,*

> *because, "God opposes the proud but shows favor to the humble."*

Humility is the polar opposite of pride and arrogance in my "humble" opinion. 2 Corinthians 10:17-18 says,

> *But, "Let the one who boasts boast in the Lord." For it is not the one who commends himself who is approved, but the one whom the Lord commends.*

Sadly, and I speak from experience, when you're a perfectionist, you experience traumatic "crashes" when things don't go as planned. You believe you did everything right, but the project failed, and you perceive that you let people down. You didn't get that job that you believed you were more-than-qualified for. And then the "old tapes" start playing ... *You're not good enough, you're a failure. If I mess up, people won't like me or think I'm all that and a bag of chips.*

The following story is a great example of when I totally lost sight of what my Companion was doing in the "Upper Story," as I was focused on my performance in the "Lower Story."

Tiny Guitar

In the late 1990s, I was making frequent business trips to Ohio. I found that when you visit an area frequently, you naturally cultivate some friendships. While working at this company in Ohio, I met a Christian woman named Barbara. We became friends over the course of my visits to this company, and she invited me to weekly lunchtime Bible studies within her workplace. I really enjoyed the fellowship of this small group. Barbara learned that I was a musician, and enjoyed singing and playing in church. During a two-week trip where I had to spend the weekend in Ohio, Barb invited me to her church and asked if I would sing a hymn for "special music." I was honored and agreed to do it. However, since I was on business travel, I did not have a guitar with me. Since I normally accompany myself when I sing, I asked Barb if someone from the congregation could loan me a guitar for the service. She spoke with someone from her church and assured me that there would be a guitar for me to use at the service.

Sunday came, and I followed the directions to this church. The building was quaint and the congregation small, yet extremely loving and welcoming. I was told that I would sing during the offering. I had prayed about it during the week and decided to sing "Amazing Grace," one of my favorite hymns.

According to the bulletin, I was scheduled to sing during the offering, after the announcements, and several congregational hymns. I had a time of fellowship before the service, but there was no mention, nor sign of a guitar. I wondered if Barbara remembered to obtain one for me? I didn't want to press the issue as a visitor, so I figured if there was no guitar, I would just sing a cappella, but I much preferred to sing with the guitar.

As offering began, I went to the platform and an older gentleman, who reminded me of my beloved "Pop," approached the stage and handed me a guitar. Although my Pop had a small guitar himself, this guitar made Pop's look like a vintage concert instrument. The guitar was tiny, out of tune, and very hard to play due to the high action. I was chuckling a bit inside and tuned it up as best I could. To me, it looked and sounded more like a child's toy.

As I started the song, I did the best I could to play the instrument. The action of the guitar was high, so I had to apply a great deal of finger pressure to produce a note, let alone a chord. I couldn't help but be distracted by the poor quality of the sound as I sang, and I wondered if I would ever be invited back again! However, when I lifted my eyes during the song, I saw an older woman in the front pew just weeping, worshipping, and soaking in the meaning of the lyrics which articulated the amazing grace of God. Shame on me; I was more focused on the quality of the music, than on what God was doing among His people. I was focused on myself and what others would think of my lousy guitar playing. But God, in His wisdom, was using an ordinary thing, a tiny guitar, (and an out-of-tune one at that), to accomplish His great purposes. Isaiah 55: 8-9 reminds me,

> *"For my thoughts are not your thoughts, neither are your ways my ways," declares the LORD. "As the heavens are higher than the earth, so are my ways higher than your ways and my thoughts than your thoughts."*

Through the years, some of my journal entries reflect my struggles with "self:"

December 5, 2010:

What are my idols? I have put a ton of idols (e.g., career, family, money, people approval, etc.) before You. Please forgive me and help me.

October 11, 2016:

Selfishness and self-centeredness. Lord I am guilty. Please forgive me and give me a heart of compassion.

October 21, 2018:

I have to stop worrying about what people think of me, the need for constant approval. Just do my best for Him, He is the One I want and need to please.

October 27, 2019:

Lord, I think deep down I worry about what others think of me. And are my experiences the "must sees" of life, i.e., the experiences others have? I compare those with mine.

For example: "So and so" went to Iceland or saw a certain group at a concert.

The wonder in life, the miracle in life, is You, living on the inside of me. The gift of salvation (eternal life), Your moment-by-moment presence, the miracle of life each day. I need nothing else. Regardless of my occupation, my financial status, my experiences, and how busy I am, You are my all-in-all, You are more than enough. Thank You for laying that truth on me this morning. You've called us to a simple life. Please help me to live that out, serving others generously and lovingly, one person at a time. Thank You, Lord.

January 24, 2020:

Fix my eyes upon Jesus, not my circumstances, agenda, abilities. I am not defined by what I do, but who I am in You.

God's Response and What I've Learned:

I'd like to say that I've overcome the sin of "me first," but I still have some growing to do. Without realizing it, I can be self-centered, self-absorbed, and selfish. To be sure, that's the way I used to live, and it is not my heart's desire to do so now.

Whether it's low self-esteem, pride, or self-reliance, when these traits manifest themselves in behavior, it means that I don't trust God. I think that this is one of the reasons that the Bible tells us to be "renewed" in our minds (Eph 4:23), because truly, our thoughts are not His! I cannot control the thoughts that come into my mind, but I can rely on God to transform those thoughts into the right perspective. 2 Corinthians 10:5 says,

> *We demolish arguments and every pretension that sets itself up against the knowledge of God, and we take captive every thought to make it obedient to Christ.*

Imagine if I applied this verse every time the "old tapes" started to play? I've found such important principles like these in the Bible that directly apply to my struggles. And so, step by step, there are some truths that I try to continually remind myself, so that I don't get trapped in focusing on myself.

For instance, I used to feel guilty about my tendency to focus on self (in either the form of self-centeredness or self-condemnation), but that guilt then became another form of self-condemnation! See how tricky the devil is? In contrast, the Bible tells us that, as believers, that's not where our focus should be. Jesus came to set us free of past guilt or shame. I love Isaiah 43:18 which says,

> *Forget the former things; do not dwell on the past.*

So instead of focusing on past "failures," Colossians 3:2 reminds me to not dwell on things in the "lower story,"

> *Set your minds on things above, not on earthly things. Set your affection on things above, not on things on the earth.*

This would have really helped me in the "tiny guitar" story! Further, the Bible confirms that it's really "not all about us." We are in a spiritual battle against the enemy of our souls, Satan. Ephesians 6:10-12 tells us,

> *Finally, be strong in the Lord and in his mighty power. Put on the full armor of God, so that you can take your stand against the devil's schemes. For our struggle is not against flesh and blood, but against the rulers, against the authorities, against the powers of this dark world and against the spiritual forces of evil in the heavenly realms.*

Think about this. The devil knows that if I am focused on me, that I can't possibly be focused on God, or others, as Jesus tells me to be. In fact, the devil is looking for every opportunity to make sure that my focus stays on self, or on the things of this world, so that I don't follow the two most important commandments Jesus gave! Look at what 1 John 2: 15-17 says:

> *Do not love the world or anything in the world. If anyone loves the world, love for the Father is not in them. For everything in the world—the lust of the flesh, the lust of the eyes, and the pride of life—comes not from the Father but from the world. The world*

> *and its desires pass away, but whoever does the will of God lives forever.*

Of course, the devil wouldn't want me to "live forever" with God. He'd want me focused on myself and the things of the world. And he's the very first one to notice an opportunity to target and tempt me in those ways. Revelation 12:10 calls the devil "the accuser of our brothers and sisters." And 1 Peter 5:8 commands us,

> *Be alert and of sober mind. Your enemy the devil prowls around like a roaring lion looking for someone to devour.*

I need to not be fooled by his schemes. My priorities need to be in the right order, placing God first, then my family, then everything else. My identity is in Jesus Christ, not in what I do for a living, or who approves of me. And because He loves me so much, nothing can separate me from that, no matter how much I think I've blown it. Even when the battle wants to rage in my mind, I can turn to the truth about who I am in Jesus Christ. Romans 8:35 – 39 confirms:

> *Who shall separate us from the love of Christ? Shall trouble or hardship or persecution or famine or*

> *nakedness or danger or sword? As it is written: "For your sake we face death all day long; we are considered as sheep to be slaughtered." No, in all these things we are more than conquerors through Him who loved us. For I am convinced that neither death nor life, neither angels nor demons, neither the present nor the future, nor any powers, neither height nor depth, nor anything else in all creation, will be able to separate us from the love of God that is in Christ Jesus our Lord.*

More than a "conqueror?" Wow. That's definitely not a label I would have applied to myself before I was a believer—at least not in the way my Companion considers it. But that's what He calls me, even when I screw it up, because nothing of this world can separate me from His love and "label" over me, as "His." And when I miss the mark, the wonderful news is that God, through His Holy Spirit, gently convicts me and has graciously provided ways for me to put others first. As I grow in my faith, God also makes opportunities clear where I can serve others and put their needs first. And there is such great blessing in loving and serving others.

Thanks be to the God who loves us; for His presence, for His patience, for the gift of salvation! May I spend the rest of my days allowing the fruits of the Spirit, and not "self," to govern my life!

> *No one should seek their own good,*
> *but the good of others.*
> *1 Corinthians 10:24*

What are your struggles with "self?"

How has God responded?

What changes do you need to make?

Chapter 12: When You Get "That" Phone Call

"I have told you these things, so that in Me you may have peace. In this world you will have trouble. But take heart! I have overcome the world."
John 16:33

In August of 1995, I was on a two-week business trip to Ohio and Diane's parents were visiting our home. We had moved from New Jersey to Pennsylvania a few years prior, which allowed us to live closer in proximity to Diane's parents. When we lived in New Jersey, Diane's folks would graciously visit and keep her company whenever I went away on business, but those trips took my in-laws between three and four hours, so this move made their commute much less of a burden at only two hours away. To this day, I am grateful for my wife's parents' willingness to help care for my family during my long business trips. At the time of this particular trip, our youngest (third) daughter was less than three months old, so the extra help was much appreciated.

Over the weekend stay in Ohio, I received a call from Diane indicating that her dad, Roger, was taken to the hospital and had an emergency appendectomy. It all happened so suddenly and unexpectedly. I immediately coordinated with my boss to arrange an early trip home. I flew home to ensure that my father-in-law's needs were met. Initially, things seemed to be going well with his recovery. Towards the end of that week, he seemed well enough to travel, so we drove my in-laws back to their home.

Just a few days later, on Saturday August 19, 1995, we were enjoying a beautiful summer afternoon at home. The kids were in the three-foot pool I had assembled in the backyard and we were planning a nice dinner. Then the call came from my in-law's neighbor indicating that my father-in-law had a massive heart attack. During the call, the medics arrived, and I asked the neighbor point blank, "Is he going to be okay?" The next words made my heart sink: "It doesn't look good." I have tears in my eyes even as I recall this memory.

Breaking this news to Diane and the kids was so difficult and painful. We quickly packed up some basic things and headed up the road to the hospital where they had taken my father-in-law, Roger. On the way up, we did not know his condition, but held out hope that he would be okay. When we got to the hospital Emergency Room and saw my mother-in-law standing there, it was clear that Roger had passed from this life into the arms of his Heavenly Father. With two phone calls, our lives had dramatically changed.

Roger was truly like a second dad to me. He loved me like a son and I believe he was grateful that I loved his little girl, his only child, more than anyone, except for the Lord Himself. Roger inspired the sentiments I have toward my own girls, and the special stewardship over my marriage to Diane. I empathized with how much a dad loves his daughter(s), and I believe he saw that in me. I had only known Roger for twelve years and it seemed like it was just too short a time.

We had a special relationship. Whenever something good was happening in my life, I couldn't wait to share it with him and he would listen intently. In fact, many times, unbeknownst to me, he would record our conversations just so he could go back and listen to every detail.

And I'll never forget his generous spirit. He was a man of very limited means, but he was always generous with Diane and me. When my wife and I bought our first house, Roger insisted on helping us with the down payment. I'll never forget what he said to me: "Bob, you need the money now, not when I'm dead." He was practical and wise. The extra money for the down payment allowed us to have a more manageable mortgage; a real blessing for a newly-married couple. And it wasn't the only time that Roger helped us. His generosity reminded me of the Gospel story of the widow's offering in Mark 12. Verse 44 says,

> *They all gave out of their wealth; but she, out of her poverty, put in everything—all she had to live on.*

I knew that Roger had put our needs before his own, and I was so grateful.

The several days after Roger's death were a blur. While we grieved, there was the reality of preparing for a funeral and ensuring that Diane's mom had the resources to continue living in her home. As sad as I was, I was placed in the immediate role of arranging everything involved in the death of a loved one. This was all new to me, and I struggled with every detail, but could not burden my wife nor mother-in-law with the arduous tasks at hand. I put on a good front, but it was so hard.

When the funeral was over, I remember coming back to my in-law's home feeling as low as I've ever felt. At that moment, nothing else mattered. Work, responsibilities, and current events in the world lost their meaning. I was heartbroken and couldn't imagine what my wife was feeling. I was at rock-bottom. Yet in spite of everything, I felt God's presence and knew that He would see us through.

A few days later, I received another phone call. This one from work. "We're sorry about your father-in-law, but it's time to come back to Ohio to continue your business trip." Life needed to go on, whether I was ready for it to, or not.

Here is my journal entry from a month later:

> **September 18, 1995:**
>
> Back in Ohio. What a difference a month makes. I can't believe that Roger is gone. Lord, You know all things. Your purpose is infinitely higher than mine. I pray for Diane, my mother-in-law, our family. Sustain us Lord.

Thank You for a safe flight. Thank You for wisdom when I feel like I know nothing relative to work. Make me a light for You.

Dealing with the Unexpected

Phone calls can be unnerving when they bring bad news. And when you're a parent (especially one like me who sometimes struggles with anxiety), or if you have aging parents, it can be tempting to worry about unexpected news. Our children are grown now, but whenever the phone rings and one of my daughters is on the line, the first thing I ask my wife is, "Is everything okay?" Most of the time it is, but sometimes one of our girls has an issue with health or work, and I tend to worry.

I remember the time when my middle daughter was in graduate school and working an internship at a nearby college. I was sitting in my office at work and my cellphone rang. I picked up and the first thing my daughter said was, "I just want you to know that I'm okay." You may be having a vicarious experience right now if your reaction is like mine was. In some ways, those are not at all comforting words and I braced myself for what was next. She explained, "I was on my way to the internship, on a busy route, and my car broke down. I was able to get off of the road but there is no shoulder due to construction. I'm in a precarious spot on an off-ramp, but I'm safe. I called AAA and they will be here shortly because I'm in an emergency situation."

I was so proud of my daughter for taking care of business before calling me, but I couldn't be at peace until I knew that the auto club was there and she was "safe." Once I received the call that she was in the tow truck, on her way to a repair shop, I was totally relieved.

Before I was a believer, I could be quickly consumed with worry and remain that way over these, and even much smaller situations. Now, I have a different set of instructions. Although I'm not perfect in following them, I quote these verses more than any others because they remind me that my peace doesn't depend on the outcome of the circumstance:

> *Do not be anxious about anything, but in every situation, by prayer and petition, with thanksgiving, present your requests to God. And the peace of God, which transcends all understanding, will guard your hearts and your minds in Christ Jesus.*
> *Philippians 4:6-7*

Uncertainty and Hopelessness

In the situation with Roger, things happened so quickly. It seemed like we had very little, if any, impact on the outcome. In 2011, I got another phone call which represented a very different trial—this time, with my own dad.

I was just about to lead an IT design review for hundreds of people from our organization around the world. I had been preparing for this important multi-day meeting for weeks. My cell phone rang and it was my mom: "You'd better get down here. Dad was at his doctor appointment and something happened. They transported him to a hospital about sixty miles away and he is not doing well. He told me not to tell you because he doesn't want you to worry."

My heart sank. Everything in front of me paled in comparison. The important event I was hosting would have to be someone else's responsibility. I had to make the long commute home, pack a bag, and drive over five hours to southern Virginia. I prayed continually on the ride down that my dad would be okay. I had no idea what I might be facing.

I arrived at the hospital and made my way to the Emergency Room where I found my mom and dad. A neighbor had driven mom to the hospital. Dad broke into tears when he saw me, and I knew that he was scared.

I spent a week at my parents' home during that time, caring for their small farm and driving my mom to the hospital, which was over an hour away from their home.

My parents had relocated from New Jersey to Virginia years ago when dad retired. They started with an empty piece of land and developed a small farm which included horses, goats, donkeys, even a llama. Having grown up spending summers on his aunt's farm in New Jersey, this was Dad's retirement dream. The little farm provided my parents great enjoyment when they were in their 50s and 60s. When dad had this medical incident though, I was forced to learn how to feed and care for the farm animals.

For me, having grown up outside of Philadelphia, I had no experience, (nor frankly the desire), to manage a farm. I knew I needed to help Mom, as she would soon take over the responsibilities that Dad had typically handled. With some instructions from Dad and a neighbor, I learned the routine—and a few critical lessons. Boots are a must; regular shoes do not work for farming. And paying attention to where you're going, also very helpful. A gash on my forehead from walking into a beam in the chicken house was the reminder I needed. Talk about a "fish out of water!"

The episode turned out to be Dad's first stroke. He had initially lost some strength on his right side, but God restored much of this over time. Aside from him also becoming more emotional, things got somewhat back to "normal" for my parents for some time. Deep inside I was still concerned about his farm, though. I knew if there was another incident, that I would have to shoulder the tasks of the farm if one, or both of them, became incapacitated. Between my responsibilities as a husband, dad, at work, and at church, there already felt like there were many people depending on me. I couldn't afford another length of time away from home and work. I was overwhelmed. My younger brother and sister assisted as well, which I was very grateful for, but they also live hours away and have busy lives themselves.

Since 2011 I've had an unspoken fear of "bad news" whenever I call my parents. In 2016, "that call" came again and this one changed my life.

I'll let my journal entries walk you through the events:

March 21, 2016:

Dad is sick and I'm concerned.

March 23, 2016: in Virginia

Life changed yesterday. Dad had his second medical incident and it's bad. Drove here at 3:45 a.m. yesterday, arrived around 9. Dad did not really know me. Goes "in" and "out." No idea what future holds with parents, job, or anything. Overwhelmed right now. Lord, please help me. Colossians 3:1 says that I have been raised with Christ, and to set my heart on things above.

A pain-free, tearless eternity awaits us.

Had a meltdown this morning while feeding animals. Dad did so much around here. Overwhelmed, but You are good.

Lord, please help me to be strong for Mom and Dad.

March 24, 2016: Day 4 of a nightmare. In Virginia.

Working on not much sleep. So much uncertainty Lord. Things need to be done at

home and I'm here. Please help me Lord. I
don't see a way out of this.

March 25, 2016: In Virginia. Day 5 of the nightmare.

Didn't sleep well last night but did wake up
without a big headache. Dad moved to rehab
yesterday. Praying for his memory, for healing
physically. I love You, Lord. Please help me to
make right decisions.

March 30, 2016:

Still in VA. Yesterday was one of the worst days
of my life. Please give me wisdom Lord. I am
overwhelmed and I know Mom is, too.

I read this prayer on social media:

Our Loving Heavenly Father,

I have been so worried about this situation. I
see no solution – no way out. But I realize that I
don't have to see the answer. I just need to
trust You to work this out in Your way and in
Your time. In Jesus's Name I pray.

After the call, when I had first arrived at the hospital,
my dad was in a small, dreary Intensive Care Unit

(ICU) room. I walked into the room, and he was sleeping and unresponsive. Mom and I sat by his bedside. Eventually a nurse woke him up. It was clear that Dad was confused and not in his right mind. As I left that afternoon to take Mom to their home, I said, "I love you, Dad." He responded, "Okay." I walked out of the room weeping, realizing that my dad didn't know who I was.

After a hospital stay of a couple days, he was transported to a local rehabilitation center/nursing home. When Dad was in rehab, he got to a point where he no longer wanted to be there. He was so used to being independent and couldn't deal with the constraints there. The medical staff told me that he was a fall risk and would likely die if he went home. This possibility frightened me, but I also couldn't stand to see my father, the strong man I looked up to, so upset and distraught. I prayed about it and felt like God was telling me to take Dad home. In my human thinking I reasoned that I would rather see him die at home, in comfortable surroundings, than in a rehab center/nursing home. While this broke my heart, I called my brother and sister to confer with them, and they agreed that this was the best decision.

The rehab center fought me and reiterated the dire risks, but I made the decision to take Dad home anyway. As I was carrying his personal belongings out of the center, I ran into a sweet lady who was part of the custodial staff. She said, "Is your dad leaving?" With tears in my eyes I said, "He shouldn't be going home, but he is so unhappy here. I don't know if I'm doing the right thing." I will never forget her words which caused me to weep and thank God. She said, "You need to take your dad home." God used the words of that sweet woman to give me peace, insofar as peace was possible at that time.

I'd like to say that everything has been just wonderful but that is not the case. Dad struggles with significant medical issues, physically and emotionally. Mom also has her share of medical issues and bears the brunt of responsibilities on the farm. I am just one phone call away from being back in Virginia to tend to my cherished parents. But God is so good. Both Dad and Mom are still with us and God has made a way for me to be in a position to help if, and when, I'm needed. I pray for my parents continually, for their well-being and relationships with the Lord. I am so grateful to still have them in my life. To God be the glory!

God's Response and What I've Learned:

I need to add this postscript to this chapter. Sometimes the right dose of humor has helped me during troubling times! My dear mother is so unassuming and, over the years, has unintentionally gotten into situations which are frankly just plain funny. For example, she has inadvertently walked into the men's room in public places, as well as a restaurant kitchen, on one occasion.

During the first day of my father's hospital stay in 2016, my mom's blood sugar was low. We had been present at the hospital for a long period of time and I recognized that mom was getting shaky; she needed food. My dad had fallen asleep and the hospital staff planned to move him from the ICU to a private room, so I informed nurses that I was taking mom out for lunch. I found a lovely little restaurant in town so we sat down to a feast of enchiladas, chips, and salsa. As we finished up, we had leftover chips and salsa, so the server bagged those up "to go." Mom wanted to call my brother and sister to furnish an update on Dad. I told Mom that I had to use the restroom, but would pay the bill and unlock my car. I asked her to get into my car, and told her I would meet her there.

I exited the restroom and looked across the dining room. Mom had left, so I walked to my vehicle which is a small, compact car. However, I did not see her there. I was about to go back into the restaurant and noticed a huge SUV parked two spaces from my car. There in the passenger seat, talking on her cell phone, was my dear mother! I panicked because I did not know the owner of that vehicle and how they would interpret this mistake if they saw an intruder in their SUV. I rushed to the SUV and opened the door. I panicked and said, "Mom, get out, that's not my car!" My sweet mother calmly hung up her phone, and slowly exited the vehicle. I thought we were in-the-clear and thought, *Whew, hopefully no one saw us!* I then asked, "Mom, where are your chips and salsa?"

She said, "Oh," and opened up the back door of the SUV where she extracted the leftover appetizers. She had actually taken the time to place the chips and salsa in the back seat, next to a multi-colored quilt.

"Mom, how did you confuse this behemoth with my little roller skate of a car? And I don't have a quilt in my car!"

Thankfully no one saw us (or if someone did, they were very gracious to not acknowledge it). That's my mom and I wouldn't change her for the world. We have a story which we laugh about to this day, and it was just what we needed on that day of uncertainty.

On a more serious note, though, even in hindsight, the foregoing journal entries made me emotional as I read them again. I saw no way out of the situation with my dad. I wondered if he would recover, and worried how my parents would manage a farm in a remote, rural area.

Now that I am on the other side of the events, precipitated by "that" phone call, what I've learned is this: Even when I'm at rock bottom, when I don't know what to do, when the situation seems hopeless, His peace is with me. He won't necessarily change the circumstance, but He changes *me within it.*

Will there be future phone calls like these? Assuming I'm still alive, the answer is yes. I'm glad that God doesn't show me what the future holds in this Lower Story, because I couldn't handle it. I am thankful for today, and trusting Him for tomorrow. I trust in His sure Word where Jesus says this in John 16:33:

> *I have told you these things, so that in Me you may have peace. In this world you will have trouble. But take heart! I have overcome the world.*

His peace, His very presence in my life, is sufficient for every trial.

My life is in Your Hands, precious Lord. I have no idea what the future holds, but You hold my future and I'm trusting You.

Have you ever received "that" phone call? What was your experience?

How has God responded?

What changes do you need to make?

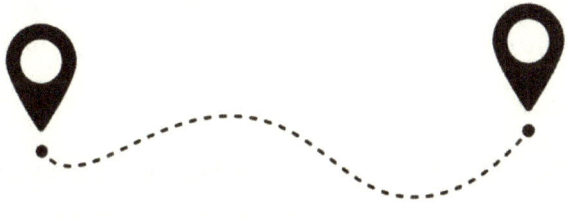

Chapter 13: Decisions, Decisions

If any of you lacks wisdom, you should ask God, who gives generously to all without finding fault, and it will be given to you.
James 1:5

In the early 1990s, we were happily living life in a small town in Pennsylvania. I had a wife, a young daughter, and a steady job. Things seemed stable, until rumors began to circulate that the workforce might be significantly downsized, and there was a strong possibility that my job would be eliminated. Jobs were not plentiful in our area. Moreover, we had a young child and a big mortgage on our home. As the provider and protector of my family, what was I going to do? We had left New Jersey and relocated to a lower cost area where we thought that it would be nice to raise a family. Now, all of that seemed like it could possibly come crashing down. At this point, I had not yet surrendered my life to Christ, nor was I journaling.

One day, I received an unexpected call from a former boss at my old place of employment in New Jersey. There was a job opening for a supervisory position and my name came up as a possible candidate. If it worked out, it would mean a promotion, and, in my mind, a good career move. I didn't ask how my wife felt about this, nor did I inquire of the Lord (there's that self-centeredness thing again). Deep inside, I felt that this had to be divine intervention because God was providing a way out if things fell apart with my current job. I made the decision to take the interview that Friday, and headed to New Jersey with my wife and daughter on the preceding Thursday night.

I didn't know how former colleagues would react to me returning for a promotion but the response was overwhelmingly positive. I couldn't deny it; the fit seemed perfect if it worked out. I would get a more prestigious title and have a number of employees working for me. Based on the lessons my dad taught me, this was a great career move and would satisfy my ambition for money, success, security, and recognition. After all, these were some of my favorite idols at the time, and I bowed down to them regularly through my thoughts and actions. The interview went well and my former boss "wined and dined" us. I was told in so many words that the job was mine for the taking. I was feeling pretty good about myself and thought that this was the ticket to significance and happiness.

There was only one problem: My wife was not on board with it at all. "Did you forget why we moved? The cost of homes and living have not gone down in New Jersey. I love where we live now," she asserted. "What about my parents? We moved to Pennsylvania to be closer to them. I don't want to move back here!"

I couldn't hear her with the noise in my head about the prestige and accolades I anticipated receiving from being a "manager." The disagreement that ensued was probably the worst one we've had in our more than thirty-five years of marriage. As it was, we had only been married for about six years when this all went down. We were at a stalemate in two separate positions. And I couldn't see past my desires and ambitions.

Sure enough, I was offered the job. I asked my former boss for a few days to decide, although I knew in my heart that I would have to turn it down. As much as I wanted the position, and everything that went with it, I did not want to live in conflict with my wife. I reasoned that I might resent her for not supporting me, but I did not want her resenting me. I decided I would take my chances, stay put in Pennsylvania, and hope for the best with my existing job. I dreaded making the call, but I turned down the position and seriously disappointed my former boss.

I kept to myself for several days, pondering the gravity of my decision. Would we survive here if my job were eliminated? Would I be happy as an analyst after the possibility of being in a more "significant" position as a manager?

Then something amazing happened. We learned that my wife was pregnant with our second child. This pregnancy was a miracle, and, though I wasn't walking with the Lord, I now know it to have been a sign from God that we were meant to stay where we were.

A few years earlier, Diane had miscarried. The miscarriage was hard on me, but traumatic for Diane—something I didn't realize until we pondered this move. We were so looking forward to a second child, and prayed for a healthy baby. We had hoped that the harbingers of a miscarriage were nothing serious, but she had issues early in the pregnancy. Unfortunately, our hopes for a second child were crushed with the miscarriage, and we had no idea if another pregnancy was even possible, let alone the subsequent risks that might come along with it. With the news of this pregnancy, after months of waiting and hoping, there was no way I could proceed to sell the house and relocate. To be honest, deep down I had no idea how we would have afforded to live back in New Jersey. The idea of "title and prestige" had overshadowed my perspective and reality.

As it turned out, God blessed us with a healthy second daughter. During delivery, there were scary moments and our pediatrician was called in during the middle of the night, but thank God, everything turned out well. In terms of work, my job was eliminated but I was offered an IT position in an organization located sixty-five miles away. Since we were settled in to our community and my oldest daughter had started school, I chose not to relocate closer to my work. This translated to more than two decades of a long, and sometimes dangerous commute. But God has been so good to us. In our small town, our children received a good education, we have a great circle of friends, and a wonderful church.

Looking back, if I had insisted on my own way and taken the job in New Jersey, it would have been the worst decision I ever made. Truthfully, our marriage may have failed because of my selfishness. I believe the road we took was the one God intended.

Everything would be different if we had taken the path I desired at the time.

So very much weighs on our decisions.

Whether we realize it or not, we make hundreds of decisions every day. Most decisions are minor, such as, "what should we make for dinner tonight" or "should I wear the blue or the red shirt?" But at other times, we face decisions that are life-changing. What is the formula for making the right decision?

The late Yogi Berra once said, "When you come to a fork in the road, take it." That is a humorous quote, but not very helpful when deciding things like, "should we sell our house and move, should I take the new job or stay where I am, should I ask this girl to marry me?" I'm sure that decisions you've made in your own life come to mind. Important decisions should not be made lightly because they always have consequences.

I love the parable Jesus tells in the Gospel of Luke:

> *Suppose one of you wants to build a tower. Won't you first sit down and estimate the cost to see if you have enough money to complete it? For if you lay the foundation and are not able to finish it, everyone who sees it will ridicule you, saying, "This person*

> *began to build and wasn't able to finish."*
> Luke 14:28 - 30

Jesus's assertion to "estimate" or "count the cost" is solid. As believers, we need to prayerfully consider if our decisions are aligned with God's will for our lives, and if they will bring glory to Him. It's not always easy to discern though; I'm grateful to know that I'm not the only one who needs confirmation of God's will in making decisions! In the Books of Second Samuel, and First Chronicles, we see examples of how King David inquired of the Lord in making some of his decisions. Here is just one example:

> *David inquired of God, saying, "Shall I go up against the Philistines? And will You give them into my hand?" Then the Lord said to him, "Go up, for I will give them into your hand."*
> 1 Chronicles 14:10

Sometimes I come to a crossroad and there is no moral right or wrong to the option I choose. Sometimes I will make a decision without much thought, and things turn out okay. Other times, I start down a road and God redirects my decisions through circumstances. However, I have also found that if I rely on my own wisdom, I might be seriously led astray.

I want to share several stories where I faced a fork in the road and needed to make a decision. Some were life-changing decisions. The last story is an example of how not to make a decision. I pray that one or all of these stories will resonate with you, and facilitate good decision-making in your life.

I Don't Want More Responsibility—but is God Speaking to Me?

In 2007, I was in charge of a major IT project which took me out of town at least once a month. I was a Project Manager with a great deal of responsibility, coupled with a "Type A" personality. These are not the ingredients for a healthy, balanced life. If you've ever worked in the IT field, you know the intensity of projects and schedules. Being in charge of a project is not for the faint of heart.

Working at a constant high pace eventually took its toll. I was used to working long hours and traveling, but wasn't getting any younger. That year in particular, I developed periodic chest pains and issues with elevated blood pressure. And then, at the peak of the project, a number of managers, including my second-level manager, planned to retire. This would open up a number of potential promotions in the organization. But even with my commitment to work,

I had zero interest or intention of applying for the second-level manager position.

First, I had learned my lesson with the New Jersey experience. At this point in my life, I honestly had no further desire to be promoted nor to have a title, and I was more than content with my income. (I realize this seems counterintuitive because many people would jump at the chance to be promoted and make more money.) Second, I had my hands full with my current position and did not want to supervise people, nor deal with personnel responsibilities. Isn't it interesting—title and prestige were exactly what I sought earlier in my career? What changed? Thanks to the Lord, I had.

As I managed my project, often on the road, colleagues and other managers encouraged me to apply for the second-level manager position. I balked at their suggestions and also thought them to be preposterous; there were other first-line managers with more experience and qualifications than I had. I also didn't have the desire, nor time, to fill out applications and administrative paperwork. Moreover, I was overwhelmed even thinking about the responsibilities of the position. There was no way that I was capable of doing the job. I wanted people to stop hounding me and hoped that things would continue as they were. (Actually, I hoped that someday life would get a little easier with less project responsibilities, not with more.) But in my spirit, I wondered if God wasn't up to something. Did He have a reason for these continued suggestions? Could He be doing something in the Upper Story and using well-meaning people to plant the seeds? How would I know? Humanly speaking, it made no sense.

In October of 2007, I had a business trip scheduled to Williamsburg, Virginia, where I would attend and speak at a three-day conference. I was prepared for the trip, but uneasy in my spirit thinking about the possibility of applying for the managerial position. I needed some quiet, alone time with God, away from distractions. I talked to my wife and asked if she would be okay if I left for Williamsburg a day early and stopped somewhere to reflect and pray. She agreed, so I left home that Monday morning and randomly stopped in central Virginia to pray and seek God's guidance. I expected (and hoped), that God would talk me out of the ridiculous idea of applying for a second-level manager position.

Selected journal entries from that time:

October 15, 2007 in Charlottesville, Virginia

Praying about/wondering what to do if promotion presents itself. The word I heard from God is, "It's not about getting rich, I am calling you to give back."

October 16, 2007, 7:15 a.m. – overnighted in Charlottesville, Virginia

I finally got to go running (praise God) last night. Praying about the future. Lord, I feel like You want me to apply for a new job when the opportunity arises—not to be rich but to give back (to bless others). Thank You for a gorgeous new day.

After a long run, followed by a long walk, I spent time in prayer with the Almighty God. The bottom line, I clearly sensed the Lord telling me to at least put my hat in the ring for the position when the job was announced. I didn't understand why, but these words kept coming up in my mind: "If I give this to you, I want you to give back."

As I said before, God had been so good and I was more than content with my current income. I didn't want more, but now I sensed God saying that, if He gives me more, I need to be generous with the increase. The financial aspect would be a blessing for sure, but it was meant to bless others as well. Still, what would the personal cost be?

Based on my encounter with God in Charlottesville, I applied for the position when the job was announced. Realistically, I didn't think I stood a chance and I forgot about the open position because my project was still consuming all of my time. Yet, subconsciously I continued to wonder if God wasn't orchestrating something bigger than what I could imagine. *Why me? I am a nobody and not qualified in any way.* Then the thought occurred to me: *God uses the weak things of this world. If He created the universe and everything in it, surely, He is big enough to help me do the impossible, if that is His will. Would God put me in a position to show Jesus to a large number of people? This may be about more than a job.* The potential influence I would have was overwhelming, yet exciting that God would consider me, for such a time as this.

Here is my journal entry after I applied for the job:

December 8, 2007:

Lord, if it is Your Will that I get this promotion, first, I cannot do it in my own strength. I need You to carry me. Help me to be a Godly leader and good example. Moreover, may my lifestyle not be larger but may I give more to Your work.

My interview was scheduled for December 14th, but I missed it due to a weather delay returning from a business trip to the St. Louis area. Consequently, I interviewed via videoconference on the following day. With the number of talented applicants, I had no expectation that I would be selected for the position. On paper, I really was the least qualified candidate and I'm not just trying to be modest. But I'll let the journal entry from December 21st speak for itself:

> **December 21, 2007:**
>
> Father, it is good to be home and have some quiet time. So much has happened this week. First, I got the call Monday afternoon that I was selected for the Division Chief job. I have been overwhelmed by the well-wishes of colleagues and I pray that I would be able to live up to the expectations of the job.

This is a journal entry from 2016, reflecting on my first few years as a supervisor:

> **February 13, 2016:**
>
> Reading my 2009-2010 journal. Didn't know how I survived two years as a second-level manager. Now it's been eight years. All You Lord.

By the grace of God, I spent almost nine years in that position. There were mornings when I would wake up and think, *Lord, how will I get through today? I have no idea what I am doing.* How did I do it? I am being totally honest: it was all God. I did not have it in me to perform successfully in that position. But in 2 Corinthians 12:9, the Apostle Paul explains it:

> *But He said to me, "My grace is sufficient for you, for My power is made perfect in weakness." Therefore, I will boast all the more gladly about my weaknesses, so that Christ's power may rest on me.*

God gave me the strength, but also used wonderful employees, colleagues, and leaders to get me through those years as a manager. God gave me the great privilege and blessing of leading about fifty people in three separate locations. The experience was much more than a job; it was all about showing the love of Jesus Christ to people. All praise be to God!

Should I Stay or Should I Go?

When my dad had his second medical incident in 2016, I was at another crossroad. I was not sure if my dad would survive one day at home, nor how my mom would deal with his health issues, or how would they manage the responsibilities on the farm. When I was on my way home, I was not sure if I would get a call and have to turn around and go right back to my parents' place. I was a second-level manager with tremendous responsibilities, and I had missed almost three weeks of work. How would I catch up? Not to mention the responsibilities with my own household.

At the end of March in 2016, after two weeks in Virginia, I left for home. Driving west on I-64 towards I-81, I broke down crying, totally overwhelmed by the circumstances. I began to pray and the Lord brought my friend Mike to mind. Mike is a trusted friend, a pastor, and a gifted guitarist. We have shared life and music together. He and his wife are two of our dearest friends. Mike and I would get together periodically for breakfast or lunch, and we would discuss our lives, and deep spiritual matters.

Weeks before my dad's medical incident, Mike and I had met for breakfast and talked about where we wanted to be in the next five to ten years. I expressed my desire to change careers at some point. Being a second level manager was intense, and my personality did not help matters. As I'd gotten older, my drive and desire to be all things to all people, had also taken their toll on my health. I never thought about leaving because I truly loved my colleagues, my boss, and my employees. Yet I knew at some point, I wanted to do something else.

I called Mike from the car. I'll never forget the conversation as I drove through Virginia. "Mike, do you have a minute? I don't know what I'm going to do. My dad is not well and I have fifty people working for me. I've got major projects with approaching deadlines. I don't even know how I'm going to handle things when I get back to work." Mike didn't hesitate with his response, which I believe came from the Lord Himself.

"Bob, you have to go…"

I think I knew that this was God's response, even before I heard Mike say it. But confirmation from a Godly brother or sister in Christ is always comforting.

Those words, ("Bob, you have to go") were life-changing and extremely scary. I had been in the same field for more than thirty-two years. For the past twenty years, I woke up at 4:30 a.m. each weekday morning and made the sixty-five-mile commute to my office. I was used to the routine. Leaving my career would be a relief for sure, but what would I do on "Day two?" How would we survive financially? Would I be letting my boss, a good friend, and my staff down, by just walking out? I knew that I wanted to do something else when things settled down in Virginia, but would I be able to find another job?

Deep down, I believed that Mike was hearing from the Lord and my decision was clear. But I still had cold feet and second guessed my decision up until the day I walked out the door for the final time. The unknown is frightening, but God continued to make me uncomfortable being comfortable.

I was also comforted by the words of Paul Stutzman, one of my favorite authors, who I mentioned in an earlier chapter. In his book, *Hiking Through,* Paul tells the story of his hike through the Appalachian Trail and the lessons he learned as he walked away from a career and into a new life. I reread this book periodically, as it has had a profound impact on my life and even helped with critical decisions I have faced. Something he wrote, spoke directly to this particular situation in my mind. Paul said,

> ... my fear of the unknown was greater than any discomfort in the present. It's why we often stay in jobs we don't find fulfilling, and why people stay in abusive situations; we are frozen in place, unable to give up our known

misery even for the promise of a happier tomorrow.[2]

That statement captured my feelings perfectly. I feared the unknown but needed to have faith that God had something bigger planned. I just couldn't see it yet, but that is where true faith comes in. Hebrews 11:1 says,

> *Now faith is confidence in what we hope for and assurance about what we do not see.*

I made my decision and formally retired from my first career in the summer of 2016. I had retirement parties at my office in Pennsylvania and in Utah. My wife compiled a memory book, unbeknownst to me, where colleagues and employees wrote kind words about me. To this day, I keep in contact with a number of these wonderful people who I consider my close friends and family. It is clear that God had a purpose for my role as a manager during that specific season in life.

God opened up my schedule to be more available for my parents which has blessed them and me. After several months, the Lord opened up a part-time job which sustained us financially and allowed me

---

[2] Paul Stutzman, *Hiking Through: One Man's Journey to Peace and Freedom on the Appalachian Trail* (Grand Rapids: Revell, 2012) 30.

personal flexibility to visit my parents. That job lasted about five months and I was out of work again. It took about five months to find another job and at times I grew impatient with the waiting. But God, in His perfect wisdom and timing, provided a wonderful full-time position where I was able to bless and be blessed by a new circle of friends. To God be the glory!

Lastly, the following is the story I mentioned earlier, as an example of how not to make a decision.

Hasty Decisions

Diane and I have always believed in helping our children get a good start in life. My dad, as well as my late father-in-law Roger, helped me, and God has placed the desire on my heart to do the same for my daughters. To that end, we passed down our used vehicles so that the girls had reliable transportation to school and work.

I was about to start a new job in July of 2017, when my middle daughter's Jeep gave up the ghost. Diane and I were driving an older Jeep with many miles and needed to upgrade to a lower-mileage car. The plan was to pass our Jeep down to my daughter, and purchase a reliable used SUV for ourselves.

Despite my good intention, one of my priorities was to make sure the car purchase happened before I started my new job and I didn't inquire of the Lord or thoroughly think things through in my haste. We did some online research and quickly began visiting used car lots. My wife saw an ad for a reasonably-priced, low mileage SUV in a town about twenty miles away. When we visited the lot, the vehicle in the ad had been sold, but we were shown a used SUV with surprisingly low miles. It was clean and roomy, and I thought it was perfect for what we were looking for. We test drove the vehicle and it ran okay for an older model. We negotiated a reasonable price and I thought that everything was good. My wife wanted to sleep on it, but I was in hurry and saw no reason to delay our decision. We paid cash on the spot, and the vehicle was ours. She drove our Jeep home from the dealership, and I operated the just-purchased SUV. On the way home, I noticed that the vehicle made a periodic grinding noise on the front driver's side, near the tire. I hadn't noticed this on our short test drive, but we didn't drive very far at that time. I dismissed the noise as "nothing to worry about," as it was an older SUV and bound to have "a few flaws."

Over the next several days, the noise became more pronounced after driving the vehicle for only a few minutes. I did some research online and was horrified to learn that this "noise" was the result of a known issue with this particular model and year. Shockingly, this defect caused radiator fluid to leak into the transmission, resulting in a grinding noise and eventual transmission failure. The fix was more expensive than the cost of the vehicle. Moreover, experts stated that the defect could cause other problems resulting in additional expenses and safety issues. Basically, I realized that we had bought a "lemon."

Instead of the quick, efficient deal I had sought, we ended up making several trips back and forth to the dealership. When we first took the vehicle back, the service department acknowledged the grinding noise, and replaced the transmission fluid. Consequently, they stated that the car was running better. I drove it home and it was fine for a few days. Then the noise returned. My wife then took the vehicle to a dealership which serviced this actual brand of SUV. The service department confirmed that the transmission fluid was already showing signs of contamination, even though it had just been changed days earlier. Basically, they also confirmed that we had bought a lemon. I couldn't possibly keep this car because it was a safety hazard, and would be cost-prohibitive to fix. I didn't want transmission failure on the highway risking my family's lives. Unfortunately, "Lemon Laws" don't apply to used vehicles, so we were in a pickle.

Even after days of heated discussions, the dealership still refused to acknowledge that the car was defective. However, they did eventually offer to take the car back if we would purchase a replacement from them. Now that I had started my new job, my wife had to assume the burden of resolving the issue. She did find a good, reliable SUV at the dealership, but at a higher price than I anticipated spending. This was our best option as opposed to the alternative. At the end of the day, we lost several thousand dollars because the dealership credited us less than we had paid for the original vehicle. But you can't put the toothpaste back into the tube.

While the dealership made out on the deal, I don't blame anyone but myself for what transpired. They could have easily refused to take the defective car back at all, which would have left us in a real financial hole. I should have inquired of the Lord and listened to my wife. I also should have been patient and done the research beforehand. Ironically, I am usually careful and thoughtful with big purchases, but I was in a hurry; I wanted this wrapped up before I started my new job. As it turned out, it took weeks to resolve and interrupted my first few days at the new job.

The old saying is true: "Haste makes waste."

Selected journal entries related to this decision:

August 1, 2017:

Start day of new job. Anxious but excited.

News on car wasn't what I expected but hopefully we can get it fixed and receive some compensation. I feel stupid for not researching more. Praying it works out.

August 6, 2017:

Lord, I pray for rest and renewal today. You are so good. Thank You for making a way with our car situation. Praying it all works out.

God's Response and What I've Learned:

There are two passages from Proverbs which I need to remember when making important decisions:

> *Trust in the LORD with all your heart*
> *and lean not on your own*
> *understanding; in all your ways*
> *submit to Him, and He will make*
> *your paths straight.*
> *Proverbs 3:5-6*

When I don't inquire of the Lord and rely on my own understanding, I can miss God's best for my life and His purposes. God also uses others to confirm the direction in which He wants me to proceed.

> *Without consultation, plans are frustrated, but with many counselors they succeed.*
> *Proverbs 15:22*

I need to seek the Lord, through prayer and His Word. It is also wise to confer with trusted Christian brothers and sisters for wisdom. And in His graciousness, when we pray in a way that aligns with His will, He reassures us that it will come to be. Jesus says in Matthew 7:7,

> *Ask and it will be given to you; seek and you will find; knock and the door will be opened to you.*

In the decisions not to move back to New Jersey, to apply for a managerial position, and to leave my first career, God provided wisdom and direction as I sought His counsel. Had I relied on my own desires, I would have missed God's best. Not only that, but I believe my life would have been totally different.

In the decision to hastily purchase a car based on my desire to get it done quickly, I lost money and caused undue stress to my wife and myself. God provided what we needed, but not without consequences.

All of these experiences and many others have taught me that I need to seek Him first in all things, especially when it comes to decisions. I need His wisdom, strength, direction, guidance, and peace. If you've never done it, I encourage you to read and meditate on Psalm 139. God created each of us and knows us intimately. What a tremendous, amazing blessing to be able to seek wisdom from the God of the universe. When we seek His wisdom, He honors our requests.

James 1:5 says,

> *If any of you lacks wisdom, you should ask God, who gives generously to all without finding fault, and it will be given to you.*

What an amazing promise!

I've also learned that my goals, desires, and ambition are secondary to God's will for my life. I need to be content with what I have, which is more than I deserve, from a loving, generous God.

I sought wealth and status early in my career and found that they do not bring joy. While my desire for those things diminished, God gave me a managerial position later in my career even though I did not ask for it.

One final, important lesson for men: Listen to your Godly wives. Things have turned out much better when I've included Diane and her wisdom in my plans. I believe that God speaks to our wives in a special way, so it behooves us to listen.

What is your decision-making process and how has it worked for you?

How has God responded?

What changes do you need to make?

Chapter 14: Wake-up Calls

And do this, understanding the present time: The hour has already come for you to wake up from your slumber, because our salvation is nearer now than when we first believed.
Romans 13:11

On our way to a much-needed vacation in the Outer Banks of North Carolina, the five of us spent the night at my parents' place in southern Virginia. This was our routine each summer; Diane, our three daughters, and myself would stop at my parents' house for a visit, and then head to the beach. The family time always blessed us as well as my parents.

When we arrived, my mom hugged me and stared at my face for a moment. I had developed a red mark on the left side of my face and it would not heal. My mother saw it and remarked, "You need to get that checked out." Now, I am not the type of person to run to the doctor for every little thing, especially since I hated to miss work for anything. I periodically cut this "mark" shaving, so rationalized that it was nothing to worry about. Moreover, because of my severe acne as a teenager, every once in a while, something would still pop up on my skin. *Just a huge pimple,* I thought. For some reason my mom was insistent, and made me promise to get my face checked out after vacation. I gave her my word and we were soon off to North Carolina for some fun and relaxation.

After returning to our home in Pennsylvania, I made an appointment to see a dermatologist, convinced that I just had an acne blotch that was being exacerbated by shaving. The day of the appointment came and I waited in the exam room. As soon as the doctor walked in, she took one look at me and said, "Honey, you have skin cancer." *Wait, what? Not even a "Good morning, Mr. Jones?"* Talk about a wake-up call!

Both fortunately, and unfortunately, I have experienced the value of several wake-up calls in my life, such as this.

Before the advent of cell phones, I would often avail myself of a "wake-up call" whenever I was on business travel. Being the driven person I am, I not only wanted to show up to work on time, but early if possible. Typically, I would call down to the hotel desk, provide my room number, and ask for a wake-up call at a designated time, e.g., 6 a.m. The call was guaranteed to wake me up from a deep sleep and ensure that I got out of bed in time for work.

As a metaphor for life lessons, I think that "wake-up calls" have also been necessary in realigning my life. I sometimes walk through this life "asleep" and need a wake-up call to get me up and going to where I need to be. Conversely, sometimes I have tried to go through this life at too high of a pace, and failed to "be still and know that He is God" (Psalm 46:10). God has used, and continues to use "wake-up calls" to get my attention. I don't know why it takes me so long to learn, but I thank God for His continued patience with me and His use of others in my life to show me His direction—such as my mom in this last story.

I've chosen to make this chapter a little different than the others, because the lessons from each "wake-up call" have been significant. I want to immediately show my Almighty Companion's mercy and presence with each one. Therefore, the section, "God's Response and What I Learned" is listed after each story. These "wake-up calls" were humbling reminders to get my priorities in order and put God first in everything.

Wake-Up Call #1: I Have What?

After the doctor announced my skin cancer diagnosis, I was incredulous and said, "I have what?" She called her associate to come in and confirm that I had basal cell carcinoma. Thankfully I learned that this form of skin cancer is treatable, but, still, the word "cancer" shocked me. I had let it go for so long that surgery on my cheek would be required.

Here are my journal entries from that time:

> **July 21, 2006:**
>
> Thank You Lord for this new day. Somehow this day seems more precious than others. Yesterday I found out that this red mark on my face is skin cancer. Fortunately, it's the most common form, but surgery will be necessary, nonetheless. With all my concern about going back to work after being off, I was not ready for the word "cancer." Yet I feel Your peace and presence more than ever. Father, use this for Your purposes and Your honor and glory. Help me know what to say about it and to whom. Blessed be Your Name.

July 22, 2006:

My life is going to be different.

Father, I praise You for this new day. It's cloudy and looks like rain but I thank You for it; thank You for a new day of life.

I slept well last night but woke up thinking about the skin cancer. What will the surgery be like? Will the scar on my face be bad?

No matter what, life will be different. I'll continue to work hard but work will not consume me. God's will, will be first, then my family, then others.

I've been a little depressed over the past two days and I hate to admit that as a Christian. I have such great memories of our vacation and I thank You for that. I cling to the passage in Philippians 4:6-7,

Do not be anxious about anything, but in every situation, by prayer and petition, with thanksgiving, present your requests to God. And the peace of God, which transcends all understanding, will guard your hearts and your minds in Christ Jesus.

God's Response and What I Learned

After the initial shock of the diagnosis and fear of the unknown, God gave me peace going into the surgery. I prayed that the pain would be minimal and God was indeed merciful. Except for the shot to numb the area, I felt no pain. I had also been concerned about scarring, especially right after surgery, when the sutures were clearly visible. It took months to fully heal, but presently, I have a barely-discernable scar.

I learned that fear is not a productive emotion. As human beings, it is normal to have fear and concern, but His Word tells us not to worry, nor to be anxious. Too many times in life I've allowed fear and worry to get in the way of joy. My Almighty Companion was present and provided peace in the midst of the storm. I also learned that the things I was focused on, such as my career and responsibilities, could all be taken away in a moment. The experience helped me to rearrange my priorities, but I did still revert back to my old ways slowly. This is a lesson I need to be reminded of continually.

Wake-Up Call #2: I Thought I Had Lost Her

On the morning of May 23, 2009, I was scheduled to play in the worship band for our church service. Just before I woke up to get ready for church, I sensed my wife tossing and turning in our bed. When I raised my head, I noticed that she was shaking violently. I had no idea what was going on, and assumed that she was having a heart attack. I quickly jumped out of bed and went to her side. The shaking had stopped, but her body was limp, and she was unresponsive. I thought I had lost her.

I immediately called for an ambulance while I cried and prayed. I had to wake the kids and gently explain that mom was having a medical issue but things would be okay, even though I had no assurance that what I had said was true. My daughters were understandably upset and scared, as I tried to hide my fear. The ambulance arrived quickly and the medics were able to wake my wife. She was able to communicate normally but was confused based on basic questions asked by the medics. The doctors diagnosed the event as a grand mal seizure of an undetermined cause. My concern was that there was an underlying issue as the cause, but subsequent tests eliminated anything serious.

Here are my journal entries from that time:

May 26, 2009 (which also happened to be my youngest daughter's birthday):

Where to begin ... off today so that Diane can see our family doctor. On Sunday morning, Diane had a seizure at about 6 in the morning. I really thought that she was having a heart attack and dying. She wasn't responding or talking. Miraculously, she gradually started to speak after the medics arrived. She seems fine and I praise You for that. I also praise You for the closeness this has generated in my family. Please let her be healed, Lord, through medicine, doctors, or just plain Your healing Hand. Please help me to adjust when I get back to work with our driving situation.

Lord, I can't honestly say that I'm passionate about my faith and am really following Jesus. That is my desire, but I'm so far away. Lord, with what happened with Diane, with my attitude, and lack of commitment to You, I need a change, I need a makeover. Diane's seizure did not seem like a good thing, but it has brought my family closer and hopefully given me perspective.

May 30, 2009:

Gorgeous day, thank You Lord. What a week it's been. I am so thankful that Diane is alive but still afraid that she'll have another seizure, and wondering if this medicine isn't having side effects. In my spirit, I sense You telling me that it will be okay, we just need to get through this. Thank You, Lord, for peace and comfort that only You can give.

God's Response and What I've Learned:

It took many months to return to a sense of normalcy. I had a fear that Diane would have additional seizures and I was obsessed with protecting her. I would go so far as to touch her in the middle of the night to make sure that she was still breathing. At some point she decided to sleep in a separate bed just so that I wouldn't worry and could sleep through the night. Since she was not permitted to drive for six months, this also created logistical issues with our jobs and gave Diane a feeling of dependency.

I didn't realize it at the time, but this event created a distance between us temporarily, something we didn't confront until years later. God spoke to both of our hearts. I had not realized that Diane was embarrassed about the seizure, and that I made things worse by being so overprotective and worried. Moreover, she interpreted my behavior as a form of anger, as if I was mad at being inconvenienced because of the seizure's effect on our routines. In reality, I was very afraid of losing my wife, thinking that her next health crisis was just waiting to happen. God's grace led me to repent and ask Diane's forgiveness. Until recently, the subject was off-limits as a discussion topic, but Diane wanted me to tell the story in this book. My Almighty Companion has healed her physically and emotionally.

This trial eventually brought me much closer to my wife and helped me to value her more. Besides the Lord Jesus Christ (who is my first priority), Diane is the most important person in my life. Above all, as a husband, I was reminded that my wife is a precious gift from God and I can never take her for granted. While I was focused on my career and providing for my family, I didn't take time to fully appreciate Diane's value as a wife and mother. I also learned that she is in God's Hands and that I need to trust Him to sustain her health and our marriage. I am so grateful for His grace and patience with me.

Wake-Up Call #3: This Can't Be Happening

In 2018, I was in my third career and had much less responsibility than I did in my first career as a manager. However, that didn't stop me from putting forth the same level of effort and intensity that has characterized my work ethic since I was a teenager. On December 10, 2018, I was at work, and was experiencing severe chest pains and several other symptoms. I had dealt with sporadic chest pains over the years, but testing always assured me that it was not a heart issue. Doctors had always explained the cause nebulously, e.g., probably muscle-related or irritated rib cage from coughing or sneezing hard. Based on the past tests and assurance from doctors, I always assumed that the chest pains were nothing to worry about. However, I'm sure that stress played no small role with the symptoms I had on this particular day.

I was sitting in a meeting at work and started to experience strange symptoms in addition to the chest pains. As usual, I assumed that things would be okay and said nothing to anyone. There was nothing going on that I considered particularly stressful, so I tried to ignore what I was feeling. Over the course of the morning though, I started to sweat, my heart felt like it was racing, and I had a pain in my left arm. I was familiar with the indicative symptoms of a heart attack and became concerned. I made it through the meeting, and walked down to the first floor of our three-story office building, and purchased a sandwich from the cafeteria. I figured that walking and getting out of the confinement of the conference room would make me feel better. I walked back to my desk and took a bite of the sandwich. I was not hungry and put the sandwich down. I just didn't feel right. I had difficulty catching my breath in addition to the other symptoms which still persisted. I was in trouble …

I tried to sit and calm down, but my body was in full panic mode. I could not control it. My first thought was to speak to my supervisor, ask for the afternoon off, and make the 65-mile commute home. I wouldn't let on that there was anything wrong. I'd just quietly leave and perhaps sleep off whatever was going on. I tried to reassure myself, thinking, *everything would be fine in the morning as it always was. I just needed to settle down and rest.* However, things weren't fine; they accelerated to the point where I thought for sure that I was having a heart attack. The last thing I wanted was to draw attention to myself, but I was scared, and didn't want to die right there in the office. I went to my boss and said, "Can you please call someone? Something is wrong." My boss calmly made the call but was told that the response would be delayed because the main ambulance was out of service. An ambulance from another town would need to respond. I sarcastically thought, *I'm glad that this isn't an emergency.* I walked downstairs and went outside, thinking that some cold, fresh air would help.

It didn't. The pain persisted and my heart continued to race uncontrollably. It felt like an eternity, but I sat alone outside until finally a rescue truck came around the corner.

When the medics arrived, they asked if a room was available inside the building. They took me inside and noticed a chair in the middle of the lobby. "Let's just do this here," one medic said. The medics removed my shirt and hooked me up to devices which monitored my vital signs. I was given nitroglycerine as a precaution and they noted that my blood pressure reading and heart rate were off-the-charts. A number of employees walked past the scene on their way to lunch, many of whom I knew. It was embarrassing as I sat there shirtless and helpless. I just kept thinking, *things like this aren't supposed to happen to me.* (There's that self/pride thing again.) But I could not control any of it. People I knew stopped by to encourage and comfort me, which was a real blessing. One woman who I had not seen in a while said, "How are you doing, Bob, good to see you!" I said, "Let me get back to you on that ..."

It's interesting to recall a conversation a former colleague and I had several years ago. We were both managers and would meet in my office first thing most mornings to discuss life, solve all the world's problems, and encourage one another. My friend would periodically say, "Remember Bob, we need to stay calm in these positions, we don't want to be carried out of here on a stretcher." We vowed that we wouldn't let that happen. Ironically, a year before this happened to me, he had a medical incident at work requiring an ambulance ride to the hospital. Now it was my turn.

Ultimately, the medics transported me to a nearby hospital in the city where I spent the afternoon and evening in the cardiac unit. On the stretcher, as the medics wheeled me to the ambulance, I remember asking God if I had accomplished all that He had planned for me because I thought, *this is it, even though I thought that You had more for me to do, Lord.* Until the first test came back, indicating that I had not had a heart attack, I seriously thought that I was going to die. I had never experienced anything like this and was sure that something was seriously wrong. I went through a series of tests and an overnight stay in Cardiac Care.

As I lay there alone in the cardiac unit with thoughts racing through my mind, I couldn't sleep. The staff had provided a slumber mask and earplugs, but there was too much activity which precluded falling asleep. At 10:00 p.m. that night I heard my cell phone "ding" with a message. I wondered who would be texting at that hour.

The unexpected text was from a former colleague in Utah. I had not seen her in years, and she apparently got my number from a mutual friend, and decided to contact me to see how me and my family were doing. (It was only 8 p.m. her time in Utah.) This colleague had recently gone through very serious health issues herself, and was able to offer hope to me. The comforting words of a friend were just what I needed. I knew it wasn't a coincidence. No one except my wife, some colleagues at work, and my middle daughter knew about my incident. I had not even told my two other daughters, nor my parents. I felt like God had used this friend to help reassure me. To this day, she still checks in on me to make sure that I'm doing okay.

Here are my journal entries from that time.

Note that the first entry was three days prior to the event:

December 7, 2018:

Thank You for life, Lord. These chest pains scare me. I am reluctant to go to the family doctor for them to tell me "it's something" or "it's nothing." Praying for Your miraculous healing Hand. I know You're able. My great Uncle Fred used to say, "If you have your health, you have everything." That's certainly true in this earthly body but, without You, I have nothing. I recall Psalm 139 – *You made and know me, Lord.*

December 12, 2018:

What a difference two days makes. Monday morning, I was praying that these chest pains would go away. Monday afternoon, I was in the ER at the hospital. Thank You, Lord, for answers. Heart and lungs are fine. I need to have follow-up doctor visits, may be reflux-related. So much outpouring of kindness from friends and family. I love You, Lord. Thank You for peace of mind. Praying for those I met in the hospital and others with not-so-good results.

I was thankful that the hospital tests did not reveal any issues with my heart, but the hospital had no precise answers for why I experienced what I did. When I was discharged, the nurse recommended a visit to my family doctor and a gastroenterologist to explore possible issues in the gastrointestinal tract. It took several months of doctor's appointments, which led to an endoscopy. My hope was that this would determine a diagnosis and rule out any type of cancer. I was anxious leading up the procedure and was expecting that "something" would be found to explain the event I had in December.

Here is the journal entry related to the endoscopy:

April 17, 2019:

Yesterday was a life-changing day after my procedure. Life-changing because God helped me, His Spirit gave me peace, and it was a wake-up call that money and work are not first. God is, then family, then everything else. Mold me and use me, Lord.

God's Response and What I Learned

As I'm sure you can tell by now, I've always been a bit of a "type A" personality. I am driven and want to give 110% at home, church, and work. This trait, "caught and taught" from my parents, has been a blessing and a curse, though. Hard work and taking responsibility are Biblical principles—however, stress is a real byproduct of this lifestyle, and I've paid a price physically, and emotionally, by not being in balance. I need to be *continually* reminded to not overcommit, and to instead, seek a life of balance. There are so many opportunities to do good things, even church-related activities, but we need to find a balance to know specifically what God wants for each of our lives.

The incident in December of 2018 was tantamount to a wake-up call by fire alarm. To say that it got my attention would be the understatement of the year. One minute, I'm an "integral" part of an organization, and an "important" participant in a meeting. The next minute, I'm helpless and hooked up to machines, believing that my life was about to end. In the hospital, I was totally at the mercy of the physicians and medical providers. But, lying in the cardiac unit that night, God's presence and peace overwhelmed me. I was humbled, and brought once again, to the realization that my life is totally in His Hands; and that the other things I rely on for security, could be taken away in an instant.

My Almighty Companion continued to give me peace and taught me patience during the four-month period between December and April, as we sought answers. I was reminded that He is with me no matter what, and that apart from Him, I can do nothing (John 15:5).

After the endoscopy, when I woke up from the anesthesia, I was surprised, but so grateful that the results were totally clean. I have occasional issues, and do have to take medication for the condition, but that is a much better outcome than it could have been. It took months to get the procedure, and I was apprehensive at the beginning. But God gave me such a peace and saw me through over four months of waiting. He was always with me.

As with the previous "wake-up calls," my Companion reminded me that He is in control, and I am not. The things I counted on, including my abilities and self-reliance, were temporary, and average at best, especially compared to Him. My peace, my strength, my very life, all depend on Him. I also learned that God uses others around us to speak hope and comfort into our lives. I want to reciprocate and provide that same hope to people in the midst of their storms in life.

In summary, these experiences were wake-up calls to slow down and not take myself so seriously. It all boils down to perspective and correct priorities. His Word says in Matthew 6:33,

> *But seek first His kingdom and His righteousness, and all these things will be given to you as well.*

I can't control my circumstances, nor my future, but my God is able to do exceedingly, abundantly, more than I could ask or imagine (Eph 3:20). I hope that I don't need more "wake-up calls" to get my attention, but He is not finished with me yet.

> *Peace I leave with you; My peace I give you. I do not give to you as the world gives. Do not let your hearts be troubled and do not be afraid.*
> *John 14:27*

What "wake-up calls" have you experienced in your life?

How has God responded?

What change do you need to make?

Chapter 15: Don't Give Up

> *... being confident of this, that He who began a good work in you will carry it on to completion until the day of Christ Jesus.*
> *Philippians 1:6*

I AM THE ONLY MALE IN MY HOUSEHOLD. We are "empty nesters" now, but at one point, I had my wife, three daughters, and two female cats as housemates. Some people have said to me over the years, "I feel sorry for you having to raise three girls," or, "Aren't you sad that you never had a boy?" Honestly, and I mean this with all of my heart, I would not have changed my family structure for anything. Being married to a Godly wife and raising three wonderful girls has been an amazing, undeserved blessing, and I consider them all gifts from God. My wife and three girls have taught me so much about life. To this day, they model love, compassion, service, confidence, perseverance, and many other positive character traits.

I want to share a story about a very challenging hike I embarked on in November of 2015. My middle daughter was in the final year of her Master's program at a college outside of Philadelphia. At her request, I drove more than two hours to pick her up to come home for the Thanksgiving break. She had planned to take a hike in the local state park near us, and I agreed to join her. I believed this would be an easy, mostly flat walk in the park. About halfway into our trip home, she asked if I was up for a challenge. I was not in the best physical shape of my life, so I asked for some details. My daughter said, "It's a five-mile total out and back hike. You can do it." That didn't sound too bad, so I concurred, and we headed to the trail.

I was not dressed for this hike, nor did I have the right shoes. I was wearing casual clothes and had a pair of running shoes on my feet. (As I learned, these shoes were not appropriate nor sufficient for what was to come!) Moreover, my daughter failed to inform me that this was a difficult, rugged, rocky trail, with steep elevation. The sign at the trailhead clued me in that this was not a trail to be taken lightly; it was a steep, rocky mountain climb. I was incredulous as I viewed the first hill, which appeared to be a straight-up climb into the clouds. However, my daughter encouraged me and said that it wasn't bad, and that the overlook, two-and-a-half miles away, would be worth the effort. The second part of her statement was true—but there was indeed a long journey ahead of me.

While hiking certain sections of the mountain, due to the elevation and rocky terrain, I had to stop and take breaks. My legs were burning, and I periodically needed to catch my breath, and rehydrate. Honestly, there were several times when I wanted to quit. As time went on, however, despite the discomfort, I was determined to finish. I came to view this hike as a metaphor for life. These thoughts crossed my mind:

If I give up on this, will I give up when other things in life get difficult?

Aren't there "mountains" in life we have to climb, and don't they seem insurmountable at times?

There's a reward to hard work and determination if I can persevere and not give up. I couldn't see the summit yet, but would miss it altogether, if I gave up now.

It took several hours, but eventually we made it to the top. As advertised, the summit was breathtaking! I could see for miles in an awesome, panoramic view.

I felt a sense of accomplishment about this climb, which helped me when I later had to make some subsequent life decisions. I was reminded that I could overcome any obstacle with God's help. I thanked my daughter profusely for the challenge. Even though she had left out a few details regarding the difficulty of the hike, it changed my life. I recently heard a saying that went something like this: "The view is worth the difficulty of the climb." I found that to be true of this hike.

Here is the journal entry from that hike.

> **November 24, 2015:**
>
> Did a 5+ mile hike with my daughter yesterday. So steep, thought of giving up. You gave me strength to keep going, and You gave me perspective about the future. You will take care of me and help me to meet any challenge. Thank You for the beauty of Your creation and precious time with my daughter.

Running Your Race

Our lives can be compared to running a marathon or embarking on a difficult mountain hike. For long races, one needs to prepare extensively and have a strategy for each mile in order to finish successfully. There are things you can plan for, but also unexpected circumstances that can, and will happen along the way. It's the same with a long, rugged hike. In any race or trail hike, you also need endurance and you must stay on the course, or you can face serious consequences. In this race of life, we need to put forth our best effort and never give up!

In this chapter, I want to focus on the lessons I've learned through running and hiking with my girls. Unlike me, they are all experienced distance runners. Their commitment to training and preparation for races always impressed me. They each ran cross-country and track in high school and college. Today, they continue to run everything from 5Ks to 10Ks, marathons, and even 50K mountain races. I've never run a long-distance race—frankly I don't have the endurance—but I understand from observation that there are obstacles and important considerations along the way such as health, weather, hills, conditions, etc. Distance races, like our journey in life, require preparation, patience, hard work, endurance, and strength. At times, the race can become difficult, and we may feel like giving up.

The Bible uses the "running" metaphor in a number of places. Here are just a few verses:

> *Therefore, since we are surrounded by such a great cloud of witnesses, let us throw off everything that hinders and the sin that so easily entangles. And let us run with perseverance the race marked out for us...*
> *Hebrews 12:1*

> *Run in such a way to win the prize.*
> *1 Corinthians 9:24*

> *I have fought the good fight, I have finished the race, I have kept the faith. Now there is in store for me the crown of righteousness, which the Lord the righteous Judge, will award unto me on that day.*
> *2 Timothy 4:7-8*

I have learned so much about life from watching my daughters run. My oldest daughter paved the way for her two younger sisters. She was talked into running by the high school cross-country coach who believed that the last place harrier was just as important as the top runner. His investment in my oldest daughter not only helped her grow and excel as a runner, but also in every aspect of life. He and his wife died tragically in an auto accident years ago, but his influence on my daughter and countless others, will live on forever. My daughter actually wrote about this wonderful coach in her college entrance essay. For her, he was a seed planter.

My middle daughter couldn't wait to follow in the footsteps of her older sister. In her first ever track meet in junior high school, she tripped and fell coming around the first turn. I cringed and hurt for her as I watched this severe fall in real-time. She eventually came to her feet and, with tears in her eyes, finished the 800-meter race. She obtained severe scrapes and burns on her knees and hands. These wounds required cleaning and bandaging, and the scars remained for a long time. The opposing coach came up to us at the end of the race and told my daughter, "That was the bravest thing I ever saw!"

Many, including myself, would have given up, and dropped out of the race after such a fall. Not her. After this experience, I figured that this would be her first, and last race, but she never gave up. She had a very successful running career in both high school and college. She not only continues to run to this day, but has also completed many difficult hikes and rock climbs in the U.S. and abroad. Running also taught her how to overcome obstacles and challenges in life.

My youngest daughter followed in her sisters' footsteps by running track and cross country. She did not display the outward excitement for running like her older sisters, but she quietly worked hard and excelled without a great deal of fanfare. In junior high, she ran the 1600 and 800-meter races. I left work early one afternoon to watch her participate in a meet at a school which was close to my office.

I became accustomed to my youngest daughter's racing strategy. She always started out slowly; and at times I wondered if she could ever move up in the pack at that pace. However, she always picked up speed gradually and exhibited a tremendous "kick" at the end. It amazed me how she methodically paced herself and gradually passed other runners to end up at the front of the pack—often in dramatic fashion.

In this particular 1600-meter race, she came on strong at the end and won the race by a close margin. As usual, I left the bleachers and met her close to the finish line. When I congratulated her at the end of the race, she was out of breath and hunched over in pain from the physical stress of the event. She sadly said, "Dad, I won't be able to recover in time for the 800, I don't feel well." To be honest, I always had concerns about my girls in the hard sport of running, especially when the weather was hot. I've seen runners faint, get sick, and often encounter serious injuries during, or after, a long race. For this reason, I told her to take it easy and that I would hang around for the remainder of the meet.

After several short races, I heard the starter pistol for the 800-meter run. As I glanced at the track, which circumnavigated the football field, I saw my daughter running in the event! She started way back in the pack, and I was concerned about her well-being based on how she felt after the 1600. But I was also so proud of her perseverance and the fact that she didn't want to let her team down. My expectations were not high since she was tired, and the 800 is more of a speed race than the 1600. I casually watched the race when, off in the distance during the final lap, I noticed a girl pass several runners as they rounded the final turn. There was my daughter, coming from way behind, to lead the race. She won by a nice margin.

Like her older sisters, my youngest daughter never gave up and persevered, even when the circumstances were difficult. Running has built character and Godly qualities into each of my daughters which has sustained them through tough times.

Take A Hike

When I was younger and someone would tell me to "take a hike," that meant that the person wanted me to "get lost", i.e., "go away." As I look back, I think that I heard that expression directed at me a lot! Thanks to my girls, all of whom are not only runners, but avid hikers as well, the phrase, "take a hike" is now a mutual invitation to get away, be active, and really enjoy God's beautiful creation together.

My girls know that my work ethic feeds the need to constantly be doing or thinking about something, and that I can easily get caught in the busyness of life. Having worked in an office environment for most of my career, I was not always in the best physical shape, as you've heard, either. I credit my girls for exposing me to the joys of hiking and "getting out" into nature. They've taught me that I have to intentionally take time off and just take a hike in order to clear my mind. And I've found that there is something therapeutic about walking through the woods, replete with streams and wildlife, nestled in the mountains. We are blessed to live relatively close to a state park through which the Appalachian Trail (AT) runs, along with other easy and challenging hiking trails.

Now, most normal people hike when the weather is pleasant. On a Friday in February of 2020, the temperature was thirty-one degrees, and I decided it was a great day for a hike. I had a lot on my mind and just wanted to take a day off from the routine. The park was empty, but there was beauty all around. A heavier coat, scarf, hat, and gloves mitigated the cold and wind. The running streams flowed beautifully and a sprinkling of snow flurries enhanced the glory of the hike. I walked over four miles, completely alone, save for the woman hiker who greeted me towards the end of my walk.

I talked to the Lord, listened, and admired the glory of His creation. I thanked Him for the ability to spend time in such a beautiful place. It took a decision and intentionality to stop and get away for a few hours, but it paid dividends. This simple time away was rejuvenating to me. Things became clearer in my mind and I gained peace about my circumstances.

If you've never just taken a hike, may I lovingly recommend the experience to you? Even though I didn't on this occasion, you'll see in this next story, it is always good to hike with a companion or two "just in case."

My Companion on the Hike

The following year, my middle daughter was home for Christmas and she wanted to run in the state park.

The weather had warmed up from previous days where we also had a little snow. The park, nestled in the mountains though, was significantly colder than it was at home. The parking lot had significant patches of ice. My daughter indicated that she planned to run a few trails. I decided to hike on part of the AT. Spoiler alert lesson: Never hike alone!

I was enjoying the beauty of God's creation, hiking a scenic trail surrounded by snow-covered trees. I didn't realize that the trail I was on had a gradual incline and increasing patches of ice. Before I knew it, I was at the top of a hill. Looking backwards, the trail was covered with ice. Looking forward, the trail was covered with ice. To my right, was a steep precipice which led to a running stream. There was no one around. I was deep in the woods, and I had to make a choice.

I chose to keep going forward. My reasoning was that the trail would eventually flatten, and I could loop back to the parking lot.

Although I was wearing good hiking shoes, and carried a walking stick, as soon as I took the first step, I knew I was in trouble. My foot hit the ice, and I slid helplessly towards the edge of the hill. There was nothing I could see to stop me, and I was quickly heading for severe injuries or possible death. I don't know how (well, yes, I do) but my body, laid flat out, feet first, miraculously stopped as my feet dangled over the edge of the cliff—as though someone had stopped me. Once again, I knew my Almighty Companion protected me from tragedy despite my bad decision. I received some bumps, bruises, and scrapes from the violent trip down the hill, but my life was spared. While the remaining trail back to the parking area was icy, it was grassy and flat, which allowed me to slowly, but safely return.

Here is my journal entry from that experience:

> **December 24, 2016:**
>
> My daughter went for a run in a local state park yesterday. I decided to hike, alone (never wise). I made my way to the top of a hill which was covered in ice. The hill had a steep drop-off and I slipped ...
>
> Thankful that You protected me on the hike where I slipped on ice and slid down a hill. Thankful I didn't go over the ledge. Would have been a severe injury or worse.

Sometimes it is good to get out of our comfort zone and not be in such a hurry. These days, I try to be intentional about taking time to listen to the Lord, and to fellowship with Him. As a result, I've seen things I never noticed before. I will share two brief, final stories from memorable walks:

1. Twice now I've walked over seven miles to pick up my vehicle from the car repair shop. Sometimes I like to "color outside of the lines," so I decided to attempt this long walk. I estimated that it would take a couple of hours, but my wife was at work and I figured it would save her the trip to take me there. I had to exercise caution on several two-lane roads but it was such a great experience. I not only got needed exercise but also saw things and encountered people I never would have if I had driven.

2. I've spent countless hours in airports over the years for business trips. In 2016, I had a long layover in Atlanta and my departure gate was located at the other end of the airport. The high-speed tram is the logical choice to get from one place to another in Atlanta. However, I had some time and decided to walk the entire length of the airport via the underground passages. During this long walk I had the privilege of observing numerous historical displays positioned along the way. It was good

exercise and, again, I saw things I never would have seen had I taken the easy way.

Time alone with God on the trail is not only good for physical health but is also rejuvenating, therapeutic, and draws us close to Him. Take a hike!

God's Response and What I've Learned:

Looking back on my own "race," I did not start out well. I was a rebellious, insecure child and teenager. I started fast, and tripped and fell early on. As I grew up, I may have looked like I was running a good race, but I was stumbling and often going off the course. At times, I could appear like a moral person, and maybe even a Christian to outsiders, but God could see my heart. I am eternally grateful for His grace, mercy, love, and patience. Deep inside, no matter how I appeared on the outside, I always felt an emptiness which no amount of reading, reasoning, or temporary stimuli could satisfy. It's been a process and a journey, and I am starting to realize the beauty in that process. He is doing a great work in my life, as though we were hiking to a summit together that has a view I simply cannot comprehend yet. Ecclesiastes 3:11 says,

> *He has made everything beautiful in*
> *its time. He has also set eternity in*
> *the human heart; yet no one can*

> *fathom what God has done from*
> *beginning to end.*

My Companion has also taught me that following Him requires faith and effort, and most times it requires doing the hard thing. As you read my stories and some of what God has done in my life, you'll see that He opened the doors, and showed the way, but I had to take the step of faith to fulfill His will. If I had chosen not to go to Texas, pursue a management position, or leave my first career when I did, I can't imagine what life would have been like. I would have missed the great view at the top of the mountain.

I'm not there yet, and can't see the summit of my life's journey, but I know that I'm headed in the right direction. My Almighty Companion is right there with me, guiding and encouraging me and I plan to finish this race strong. How? Through Him who gives me strength.

> *I can do all this through Him who*
> *gives me strength.*
> *Philippians 4:13*

> *His divine power has given us everything we need for a godly life through our knowledge of Him who called us by his own glory and goodness.*
> *2 Peter 1:3*

No matter how we start, it's all about overcoming challenges, persevering, and finishing well. Even though I've stumbled, even though you may have stumbled, we have the greatest resource anywhere, the Lord Himself. He has promised to go with you. Take the first step and be prepared for challenges. Persevere. The view will be spectacular! Never give up.

> *For physical training is of some value, but godliness has value for all things, holding promise for both the present life and the life to come.*
> *1 Timothy 4:8*

How are you doing in your race?

What is God's response?

What changes do you need to make?

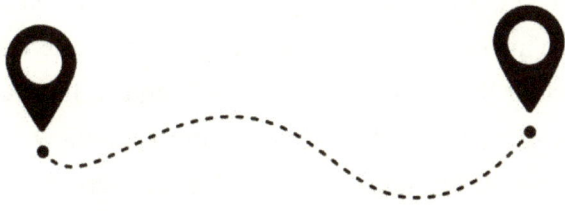

Chapter 16: Where Do We Go from Here?

> *God again set a certain day, calling it "Today." This He did when a long time later He spoke through David, as in the passage already quoted: "Today, if you hear his voice, do not harden your hearts."*
> Hebrews 4:7

W E'VE COME TO THE END OF OUR TIME TOGETHER IN THIS BOOK, but our journeys continue beyond these pages. As you've read, my life took on two different paths. Until I was about thirty years old, I was on a trail which led me away from God. I enjoyed many things on the trail, but also travelled down many dangerous, sinful paths which got me into trouble. One day, God lovingly tapped me on the shoulder and gently led me to a new, narrow path. This path has not been easy, but it is the way of abundant life. I know my story will end well because I'm on the path leading to that wonderful view from the summit. I'm not sure when I'll get there, but I know that when I do, I'll see Jesus face-to-face.

So, what is your story and how is your journey going? Is your journey one of hope? Are you perhaps exhausted, as a dad, a husband, a wife, a mother? Do you worry about how you measure up to others? Do you talk one way but live another? Do you know that you need to change, but feel powerless to do so? Are you consumed with work or maybe worried about how you will put your kids through college? Are you a positive person or a skeptic? I ask these questions because they permeated my own story. If some of these things hit home with you, know that you're not alone, and there is hope!

First Things First—While It Is Today

The Bible indicates that there are two roads in life; a broad road and a narrow road. The narrow road leads to eternal life with God. The broad (wide) road, the one I walked for so many years, leads to eternal separation from God. Matthew 7:13-14 says,

> *Enter through the narrow gate. For wide is the gate and broad is the road that leads to destruction, and many enter through it. But small is the gate and narrow the road that leads to life, and only a few find it.*

As a friend, I lovingly ask you, "Which road are you on? Are you on the path to life or destruction?" Each one of us needs to make a choice. Which road will we choose?

For those of you who have never considered the free gift of salvation through Jesus Christ, I would like to share the greatest truth I've ever learned: God loves me, and you, more than we could ever fathom. He came into this broken world because of His love for us, and gave His life for our sins. Maybe you're hearing this for the first time, or perhaps you have heard it but have never considered it.

According to the Bible, we are all sinners and deserve God's judgement. Romans 3:23 tells us,

> *... for all have sinned and fall short of the glory of God.*

You may believe, as I did, that you are basically a good person and have no need of a Savior. However, "basically good" is not good enough. Let me explain.

God does not grade on a curve. We may look good in our own eyes compared to someone else, but our view is tainted.

Picture the Grand Canyon and imagine yourself on one rim, and God on the other. The only way to God is to jump across the chasm. You may make it a little farther than I would, but we both would still fall *way short*. That is how it is; God is absolutely holy and sin cannot enter His presence. We couldn't make it on our own even if we gave it our best effort. Sin requires death, physically and spiritually. We could never do enough good deeds or acts of service to earn God's favor. That's why God the Father sent Jesus, His only Son, to rescue us. Romans 6:23 says,

> *For the wages of sin is death, but the gift of God is eternal life in Christ Jesus our Lord.*

And John 3:16, perhaps the most quoted verse in the Bible, captures the Gospel message succinctly:

> *For God so loved the world that He gave His one and only Son, that whoever believes in Him shall not perish but have eternal life.*

The Bible confirms that Jesus is the only way to eternal life. Acts 4:12 says,

> *Salvation is found in no one else, for there is no other name under heaven given to mankind by which we must be saved.*

We must make a decision to receive God's free gift of salvation through Jesus Christ. John 3:17-18 says,

> *For God did not send his Son into the world to condemn the world, but to save the world through Him. Whoever believes in Him is not condemned, but whoever does not believe stands condemned already because they have not believed in the name of God's one and only Son."*

And John 3:36 states,

> *Whoever believes in the Son has eternal life, but whoever rejects the Son will not see life, for God's wrath remains on them.*

Here is the bottom line, dear friend: None of us knows how long we will live on this earth, and tomorrow is not guaranteed. Deep down we all realize that this life on earth is temporary. The fact is, we don't know if we have ten years, one year, or even one more minute of life. James 4:14 says,

> *Why, you do not even know what will happen tomorrow. What is your life? You are a mist that appears for a little while and then vanishes.*

Hebrews 3:15 says,

> *As has just been said: "Today, if you hear his voice, do not harden your hearts as you did in the rebellion."*

My friend, I care deeply about you, whether we've actually met, or not. I wrote this book to give people a message of hope. If you don't know Jesus Christ personally, if you have never admitted that you are a sinner and asked for His forgiveness, I lovingly implore you to do so. Romans 10:9 says,

> *...that if you confess with your mouth Jesus as Lord, and believe in your heart that God raised Him from the dead, you will be saved.*

Belief is more than acknowledgement; it's putting your total trust in Jesus Christ to rescue you and forgive you of all your sins. It's the greatest gift ever given! We receive it. And then we take steps to live out that love.

I made the decision to surrender my life to Jesus in the early 1990s, standing by the New Jersey Turnpike. Wherever you are, you can make that decision right now by praying a prayer like this, from your heart. Your Almighty Companion will be right there to hear it:

Lord God, I know that deep down I am a sinner. I admit that I have sinned in my thoughts, in the words I've said, and things I've done. I confess those things to You and ask for Your forgiveness. You love me so much that You sent Your Son Jesus Christ, God in the flesh, to die in my place, to shed His precious blood and make the perfect sacrifice for my sins. I turn from my sins and receive Your precious gift of eternal life. Thank You for dying for me, thank You for raising Jesus from the dead to give me the certainty of eternal life with You. Please go with me in this journey and help me to live a life pleasing to You. In Jesus's Name.

If you gave your life to Christ through this prayer, please tell someone. This is the first step to following Him. God wants to draw you deeper into a relationship with Him and help you to grow. The enemy (Satan), will do everything he can to draw you away from Jesus and he will waste no time in doing it. Contact a pastor at a local church or ask a Christian friend to help you. They will assist you in obtaining a Bible and anything you need to grow in your relationship with the Lord. None of us is an island. We need brothers and sisters in Christ to sharpen us and keep us accountable. I also recommend that you read the Gospel of John with an open heart and childlike faith. John provides a wonderful picture of who Jesus is, and what He has done for each of us.

Here are several verses to encourage you with your decision.

> *Therefore, since we have been justified through faith, we have peace with God through our Lord Jesus Christ.*
> *Romans 5:1*

> *Therefore, there is now no condemnation for those who are in Christ Jesus.*
> *Romans 8:1*

Still Skeptical?

If you recall the details of my story, I was a confirmed skeptic. In some ways, I still am; I don't readily accept what I hear at face value, especially these days where everyone seems to have an opinion. I require proof, and more than just a talking point before I'll accept something as "truth."

So perhaps you've heard all of the claims and still make the conscious choice to reject Jesus Christ. Please indulge me for a moment and allow me to share some of my own previous arguments against Christianity, before I understood differently. You may relate to some of these points, as I used to.

I'm a "good" person and have no need for a Savior. Life is great, I've got what I need. My faith is my career, position, appearance, (or fill in the blank).

Those things I relied on for meaning worked well for me, until they didn't. When the things I relied on were shaken, I realized that I was not in control of my destiny. I had very little power to do anything on my own—including to sustain my very life.

My belief system is eclectic. I'm part atheist, agnostic, or another religion or movement.

Been there, done that. I'm not saying you do, but speaking from personal experience, I felt pretty smart and superior when I pulled principles from different sources. But I found that the claims were not based on foundational truth. I also basically lived as a "practical atheist" during the times I sat in church but walked a path that led away from God. It led me nowhere truly satisfying. All of the holes were still there, even if they were hidden away in philosophy and explanation. Had

I held on to my misconceptions, I would have been eternally lost.

I am going to live as I please, I'll get right with God later, I have lots of time.

As we've discussed, that is a foolish worldview because none of us knows how long we have. In Luke 12 there is a parable about a rich man who had an abundance of crops, which translated to wealth. He made plans to build bigger barns to store his abundance and surplus. Verses 19-21 nail down the conclusion of the matter:

> *And I'll say to myself, "You have plenty of grain laid up for many years. Take life easy; eat, drink and be merry."' But God said to him, "You fool! This very night your life will be demanded from you. Then who will get what you have prepared for yourself?" This is how it will be with whoever stores up things for themselves but is not rich toward God.*

Wow, this is how I viewed life in my younger years. I didn't think about the fact that tomorrow may never come.

I attend church so I'm "covered" with God.

Been there, done that, too. I sat in church sporadically for many years and did not know Jesus Christ. Ever heard the saying, "Sitting in church doesn't make you any more a Christian than sitting in a garage makes you a car?" While I love my local church and the encouragement it provides, the Christian life is not about "church." Church cannot save you. It's about a relationship with Jesus Christ and "being the church" to those around us.

My circumstances are too painful and unbearable. If God really existed, He would remove all of that.

This is a tough one, because my heart breaks for family, friends, and people I hear about who are going through difficult trials. I pray and intercede for those going through difficult times. I try never to say to someone, "I know what you're going through" because I don't walk in their shoes, even if I've been through something similar. In my own experience, God has not always taken away the pain or the circumstances. But I don't know where I would be without His presence, and His peace in those storms. I humbly leave you with several verses from God's Word and I pray that you are encouraged:

> *In all this you greatly rejoice, though now for a little while you may have had to suffer grief in all kinds of trials.*
> *1 Peter 1:6*

> *... if this is so, then the Lord knows how to rescue the godly from trials and to hold the unrighteous for punishment on the day of judgment.*
> *2 Peter 2:9*

> *For our light and momentary troubles are achieving for us an eternal glory that far outweighs them all.*
> *2 Corinthians 4:17*

I'm too far gone for God to forgive me.

I felt that way at the height of my lifestyle in the music world and I look back with regret over those life choices and sins. But His Word tells us that we are never too far gone. God loves us so much that He sent His Son Jesus to die for us. I love this verse in Luke 15:10,

> *In the same way, I tell you, there is rejoicing in the presence of the angels of God over one sinner who repents.*

The church is full of hypocrites.

This is a popular one—and one I used to use regularly. Let me first say that I agree with you! It was true when I was not following Jesus, and it's true today. The church does contain hypocrites, people who appear one way, who say one thing, but act another way. Honestly, I can be a hypocrite sometimes as well. But here is the deal: This is not about church or religion, it is about a relationship with the living God through Jesus Christ. Hypocrites need Jesus as much as anyone! And honestly, in addition to my own mirror, I discovered hypocrites in the workplace, at the local coffee shop, at the bank, and at the supermarket. But that did not stop me from going to those places. I just used this as an excuse.

Above all, I have let people down at times and others will do that too, believer or non-believer. We still have that sin nature that rears its ugly head. Jesus, however, is the best friend you could ever have. He will never leave or forsake you. He made that promise to those who put their trust and hope in Him. And if He is your Almighty Companion, as He is mine, He goes with you, into the workplace, the coffee shop, the bank and even into the group of hypocrites. After all, Who better to take right into the heart of these everyday situations?

My worldview and belief system "work" for me. I tried Christianity and it didn't feel right.

I can relate to this one, too. My eclectic belief system "felt right" back in my college years. It "worked" for me (kind of). I even justified some of my sins based on the books I read. As long as it felt good and I "wasn't hurting anyone," my conscience was clear (but it really wasn't). Feelings can be helpful but we can't rely on them when it comes to seeking truth. And the truth was, that my sin was hurting others all around me whether I wanted to admit that or not.

I remember the time when my wife and I returned from the East Coast to Texas after celebrating Christmas. Before we departed to the East Coast for Christmas, I left my car at a friend's house and he drove us to Dallas-Fort Worth (DFW) Airport. When we flew back to Texas, we rented a car at DFW and drove it to my friend's house to pick up my vehicle. From there, Diane (who was my fiancée at the time), drove the rental car and followed me back to the interstate. The plan was to return the rental to our local airport in East Texas. It was very dark out and I entered the interstate to make the remaining hour-long drive to East Texas. I had driven for several miles when I noticed a sign: "Dallas–100 miles." My feelings had failed me. I thought for certain that I was headed home, to my desired destination. But I was actually heading in the exact opposite direction. If we rely solely on our feelings we can easily be misled. Proverbs 14:12 says,

> *There is a way that seems right to a man, but in the end, it leads to death.*

You know what the hardest thing was for me? Giving up control of my life to someone else, as if I really had control. I don't like not being in control of my circumstances, and surrendering my life to Christ, and trusting Him completely, was frightening. When you think about it though, we have very little control. Just look at our world in the year 2020.

I don't know if you can relate to any of the aforementioned arguments, but I wrestled with these myself. I hope that you will honestly consider the validity of the Bible and claims of Jesus Christ, and not just blow them off because of preconceived notions. In your heart of hearts, do you know for sure that you are on the path to life?

Before I surrendered my life to Jesus Christ, I examined and considered a plethora of religions and belief systems. When I finally investigated the credibility of the Bible, I found that it stands apart from any other book. The evidence that man has discovered in history and archaeology is overwhelming. There is no other book like it, and I believe that it is the inerrant Word of God. It has stood the test of time and scrutiny, even though people today will still criticize and make false claims about its legitimacy. I am not a Biblical scholar, but there are plenty of sources, from learned Christians and secular experts, you can check out for yourself. When I finally surrendered my life to Him, I read through the Bible and began to learn and grow through its truths. I continue to grow in my faith and relationship with Jesus each day by studying and meditating upon His Word.

I also studied the claims of Jesus. In Matthew 16, Jesus asks crucial questions about Himself. Here is the account in verses 13- 15:

> *When Jesus came to the region of Caesarea Philippi, He asked his disciples, "Who do people say the Son of Man is?" They replied, "Some say John the Baptist; others say Elijah; and still others, Jeremiah or one of the prophets."*

> *"But what about you?" He asked. "Who do you say I am?"*

In today's culture, some say that Jesus was a moral man and a good teacher. Certainly, He was all of that, but He also claimed to be God. Verse 16 goes on to say:

> *Simon Peter answered, "You are the
> Messiah, the Son of the living God."*

And Jesus responded by confirming that Simon Peter was blessed to know this truth.

What about you? *Who do you say He is?*

I love people and respect other traditions and religions, I really do. I have learned so much from interacting with friends of other faiths and those who don't believe in God at all. I love getting to know people and understanding their worldviews and backgrounds. Having said that, as a friend, I want to lovingly challenge you with a question, one I wrestled with myself: Can your worldview, your philosophy, your belief system get you to the right destination? Can it save you? Can you be sure? With all due respect for the various religions, philosophies, movements, and opinions in our world, there truly is only one way to God; only one path to get us home to our ultimate destination. John 14:6 says,

> *Jesus answered, "I am the Way and
> the Truth and the Life. No one comes
> to the Father except through Me."*

Some may argue that the Bible is too exclusive, e.g., "it doesn't make sense that there is only one way to God." In reality, I believe that it's just the opposite: The Bible is totally inclusive. Jesus invites *everyone* to come to Him. John 1:12 says

> *Yet to all who did receive Him, to those who believed in His name, He gave the right to become children of God.*

There is irrefutable evidence that Jesus actually lived, He really died, and was really raised from the dead. If all of that is true, we have a choice to either believe, and follow, or—reject those claims. *Who do you say He is?* I invite you to check it for yourself with an open mind. You don't have to check your brains at the door to take an honest look at Christianity. Remember, I am a skeptic at heart, but one who professed to being open-minded. Therefore, it would have been disingenuous of me to simply write off the Bible, and claims of Jesus without truly investigating those things for myself.

> *Seek the LORD while He may be found; call on Him while He is near.*
> *Isaiah 55:6*

Alright. Why did I take the time to tell you all of this? Because I want to proclaim the love of Jesus to everyone I meet. He is the reason for my hope as I told you earlier in my story. His Word says in 1 Peter 3:15,

> *But in your hearts revere Christ as Lord. Always be prepared to give an answer to everyone who asks you to give the reason for the hope that you have. But do this with gentleness and respect.*

I want to spend the rest of my days living for Him according to His Word. I know that I can't do it perfectly because I still live in this body which has a sin nature. But I also have the Holy Spirit, my Almighty Companion who helps me navigate this trail and head the right way when I stray off of the path. Maybe you're searching and tired of running. Jesus is waiting to receive you. Please call to Him while it is today. There is no better decision you'll ever make.

For Those Who Claim to Follow Jesus Christ

If you fall into this category, as I do, I am going to make you a little uncomfortable. Please know that my goal is not to be judgmental, but to see how you're doing on your journey. Remember those "pop quizzes" back in high school? The purpose of those was not just to annoy the students, but to check for evidence that we had learned what we were taught. 2 Corinthians 13:5 says,

> *Examine yourselves to see whether
> you are in the faith; test yourselves.
> Do you not realize that Christ Jesus is
> in you—unless, of course, you fail the
> test?*

There is value to assessing our walk with Jesus to ensure that our eyes are fixed on Him, and that we are truly living for Him.

If you have surrendered your life to Jesus Christ, and trusted Him for Your salvation, you know that you have received the best gift there is! Whether you were five, or eighty-five years old when He rescued you, you are His precious child. Our destination on this journey is eternity in His presence but He also promises abundant, eternal life right now! We have a relationship with and access to the living God! It's truly amazing.

So how is your journey going? If your journey is going well, congratulations, I praise God for that! Are you walking with Jesus daily, or are you struggling? Maybe you've veered off of the path and need a little encouragement to get back on the trail. Sometimes when I am on a mountain hike, I'll look back to see how far I've come. It's amazing when I see a steep hill I've just climbed, reminding me that I'm close to the summit. It's good to take stock of our walk with Jesus to see how we're doing. My journals help me to do that when I get discouraged and think that maybe I've slipped too far. Remember that Satan will also try to push us off of the narrow path. Know that God's Holy Spirit lives within us and He is always our faithful Companion on the journey, keeping us on the right path as we fix our eyes on Him.

I want to end our time together with a quick look at a passage from Galatians 5. I think that it summarizes the Christian walk well and gives us tools for our journey. Verses 13 – 26 say this:

> *You, my brothers and sisters, were called to be free. But do not use your freedom to indulge the flesh; rather, serve one another humbly in love. For the entire law is fulfilled in keeping this one command: "Love your neighbor as yourself." If you bite and devour each other, watch out or you will be destroyed by each other. So I say, walk by the Spirit, and you will not gratify the desires of the flesh. For the flesh desires what is contrary to the Spirit, and the Spirit what is contrary to the flesh. They are in conflict with each other, so that you are not to do whatever you want. But*

> *if you are led by the Spirit, you are not under the law.*
>
> *The acts of the flesh are obvious: sexual immorality, impurity and debauchery; idolatry and witchcraft; hatred, discord, jealousy, fits of rage, selfish ambition, dissensions, factions and envy; drunkenness, orgies, and the like. I warn you, as I did before, that those who live like this will not inherit the kingdom of God. But the fruit of the Spirit is love, joy, peace, forbearance, kindness, goodness, faithfulness, gentleness and self-control. Against such things there is no law. Those who belong to Christ Jesus have crucified the flesh with its passions and desires. Since we live by the Spirit, let us keep in step with the Spirit. Let us not become conceited, provoking and envying each other.*

I want to focus on several points in the foregoing passage. The acts of the flesh should not be characteristic of our walk. The fruit of the Spirit should reflect who we are in Jesus Christ. Notice that we are to serve one another humbly in love. And, God's entire law is fulfilled in keeping this one command: "Love your neighbor as yourself." Putting others first, and loving our neighbors should be our response to His great love.

I know from my own experience that these things do not come naturally. I was not a loving, kind, self-controlled person before Jesus saved me. Sometimes, even now, I get off of the path and exemplify the opposite of joy, forbearance, et. al. But my Companion is there to gently move me back to the path so that I can continue towards my destination.

In this exam, however, I need to get very personal with myself and you: Does my speech, verbal or otherwise, reflect the fruit of the Spirit? Is my character and behavior drawing people to Jesus Christ or pushing them away? John 3:8 tells us to,

> *Produce fruit in keeping with repentance.*

The way to stay on the path is to seek God, listen to Him, and study His Word continually. That is why the Bible is my playbook, that is why I record notes in my journal. Spending time with the Lord, daily and intentionally, is a valuable discipline that will keep us on the right path and take us to our glorious destination with our wonderful Lord and Savior.

One Last Bob Story

We've talked about some serious stuff. The truth is, it doesn't get any more serious than making a decision about where to spend eternity. So before I end, I want to lighten up it for a moment and leave you with one last "Bob" story that will hopefully make you laugh.

I made a number of trips to the St. Louis area towards the end of my first career, in the 2015-2016 timeframe. When you travel a great deal, certain things become routine, such as renting a car. Whether the cars were located on the airport property, or in a remote lot, the process was basically the same and I performed it by rote. (Is it any wonder that I left my license in the Chicago area for a month?) It was a Sunday afternoon when I landed in St. Louis and shuttled to the rental agency.

Once I completed the paperwork and the clerk swiped my credit card, I was informed that my vehicle was in an assigned slot in the large parking lot. The clerk also told me that my car had keyless entry and start capability. That was something new to me and I didn't bother to ask any details (again, I was blindly following my routine). Even though I worked in the Information Technology (IT) field for years, I am still somewhat clueless when it comes to modern technology. I'm grateful to have kids who can explain the latest technical things to me! (In this instance, though, my kids were not with me.) As I walked through the lot to locate my vehicle, I wondered how this keyless thing worked because I did not receive a key or fob to start the car.

When I located my car, right where it was supposed to be in the assigned slot, I found it unlocked. I routinely opened the driver-side door and tossed my carry-on bag into the front passenger seat. I then placed my suitcase in the backseat. Lastly, I placed my derriere into the driver's seat. I was so comfortable with my routine!

I noticed a button in the dash which indicated, "Press to Start." So, I did. Nothing happened. I scratched my head for a moment and then saw a display in the dashboard which indicated, "Hold down brake pedal and press start button." Ah, magic! As I pressed the brake and pushed the button, the engine began to purr. *This is so cool,* I thought, as if I just discovered some unexplored territory.

As I backed out and then proceeded to the gate where an associate checks paperwork, a thought crossed my mind: How will I lock and unlock the car when I park it at the hotel? There is no key or fob. I approached the gate and the associate said, "Good afternoon, may I see your paperwork?" I complied and everything was in order. I then asked her the question I had been pondering, "Shouldn't I have a key or something to be able to lock and unlock the car?" She smiled and said, "You should have a key fob in the cupholder; you couldn't have started the car without it."

Hmm... I checked the cupholder, nothing. She asked me to check the storage area on the passenger door. I leaned over to check the passenger door and, as I did, the woman politely remarked, "Sir, you're sitting on it." Really? Somehow, in my routine, I had not noticed the fob on the driver's seat whenever I entered the car. I was focused on tossing my carry-on bag to the passenger seat. How did I miss it? I sheepishly said to the associate as I pulled away, "Now you have a funny story to tell your family at dinner—how the clueless man from Pennsylvania did not know how a keyless start car functions, nor that he was sitting on the fob!" And who would ever guess that I worked in IT for a living!

The answer was right underneath me. I hope by now you have heard that this has often been the case in my life. Perhaps the answer you're seeking is not far from you either, my friend.

Final Word

I gave you a "BLUF" at the beginning of this book: Fix your eyes on Jesus and follow Him. That is not a guarantee of prosperity or success. It's my response to what He has done, no matter what I go through in this "Lower Story."

We are living in times where everything from disease, injustice, anger, hatred, violence, division, and negativity abound. It seems like each day there is something else in the news which makes us wonder what is happening to our world. These events cause anxiety, even in followers of Jesus Christ. The truth is, we live in a broken world and we all need hope. This is nothing new and we've seen these things play out in history. I believe that our 24/7 news cycle, the internet, and social media make us more aware because we are bombarded with information and opinion.

If you're overwhelmed by all that is happening, I want to encourage you and let you know that there is hope, and you are not alone. God loves you and is working in the Upper Story in ways that we cannot see. No one is out of God's reach.

I hope that you've been encouraged by the journal entries and stories. I also hope that you'll consider the joys of journaling and a daily quiet time with the Lord. It will give you a beautiful glimpse of the summit to come. Above all, I pray that you will draw closer to our Lord and Savior, Jesus Christ. Fix your eyes on Jesus and follow Him!

I love the account in the Gospel of Luke where Jesus tells the story of two people who were indebted to a moneylender. One owed a tremendous amount of money and the other had a smaller debt. Neither had the means to pay the money back; but the moneylender forgave both debts. Jesus then asks Simon Peter "Now which of them will love him more?" and Simon replied, "I suppose the one who had the bigger debt forgiven." "You have judged correctly," Jesus said (Luke 7: 42-43).

The foregoing passage speaks to me because I have been forgiven so much. Imagine having a million-dollar debt you could never pay back. One day you receive a letter from the bank: "Your debt has been paid in full. Just sign here to receive it." That's what Jesus did for each of us; we can have our debt paid and our sins forgiven, if we will place our trust in His finished work on the cross.

Whether you're someone who is very successful and well-known, or just an "average" person like me, we have an Almighty God who loves us, answers our prayers, and walks with us through every situation. He can take the messiest life and turn it into something beautiful. I am the least of people, average at best, but rescued from a life of sin, to a life of joy with my Savior!

It bears repeating: Jesus is the reason for my hope and I pray that you have discovered that same truth. He has done everything for me and I could never do enough to repay Him. My response is to finish this journey faithfully, loving and serving others, and walking with my Almighty Companion to eternity—where the view will be spectacular!

God bless you and thank you for reading.

Until we meet again, your friend,

Bob

> *He lifted me out of the slimy pit, out of the mud and mire; He set my feet on a rock and gave me a firm place to stand. He put a new song in my mouth, a hymn of praise to our God. Many will see and fear the LORD and put their trust in Him.*
> *Psalm 40:2-3*

The LORD is not slow in keeping His promise, as some understand slowness. Instead He is patient with you, not wanting anyone to perish, but everyone to come to repentance.
2 Peter 3:9

Then Jesus said to his disciples, "Whoever wants to be my disciple must deny themselves and take up their cross and follow me."
Matthew 16:24

About the Author

Bob Jones is an average guy from New Jersey who decided to write a book based on almost three decades of journaling. Years of marriage and leadership in a large organization shaped stories on a journey that continues to this day. His goal is to share these stories with men and women everywhere who are searching for hope. Bob is the father of three amazing grown daughters and lives in Central Pennsylvania with his much-better-than-average wife. In addition to writing, he enjoys music, hiking, reading, and sharing the love of Jesus Christ with anyone who asks. Connect with Bob online at saxmanRJ7509@gmail.com or on social media.

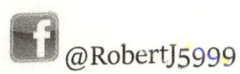 @RobertJ5999    @BJRJ5999

Additional copies of this book, now available at Amazon.com or BarnesandNoble.com.

Get one for the "average" guy in your life.